LORENZACCIO
A DRAMA IN FIVE ACTS

BY

ALFRED DE MUSSET

(1833.)

DONE INTO ENGLISH BY
DR. EDMUND BURKE THOMPSON

(1905.)

Edited by
B. K. De Fabris

Timeless📖Classics

CHARACTERS:

ALEXANDER DE MEDICIS, *Duke of Florence.*
LORENZO DE MEDICIS *(LORENZACCIO)*, *Duke's Cousin*
COSMO DE MEDICIS, *Duke's Cousin*
CARDINAL CIBO.
THE MARQUIS OF CIBO, *his Brother.*
SIR MAURICE, *Chancellor of the Eight.*
CARDINAL BACCIO VALORI, *Apostolic Deputy.*
JULIEN SALVIATI.
PHILIPPE STROZZI.
PIERRE STROZZI, *Philippe's Son*
THOMAS STROZZI, *Philippe's Son*
LEON STROZZI, *Philippe's Son, Prior of Capua,*
ROBERTO CORSINI, *Purveyor of the Fortress.*
FRANCOIS PAZZI.
ALAMANNO SALVIATI, *Republican Noblemen.*
PALLA RUCCELLAI, *Republican Noblemen.*
BINDO ALTOVITI, *Uncle of Lorenzo.*
VENTURI, *a Citizen.*
TEBALDEO, *an Artist.*
SCORONCONCOLO, *a Bully.*
COUNCIL OF THE EIGHT.
GIOMO THE HUNGARIAN, *the Duke's Equerry.*
MAFFIO, *a Citizen.*
MARIE SODERINI, *Mother of Lorenzo.*
CATHERINE GINORI, *his Aunt.*
THE MARQUISE OF CIBO.
LOUISE STROZZI.

Two Ladies of the court and a German Officer, a Goldsmith, a Mercer, two Preceptors and two Children, Pages, Soldiers, Monks, Courtiers, Exiles, Students, Servants, Citizens, etc., etc.

The Scene is at Florence.

ACT THE FIRST

SCENE I

(A garden. Moonlight. A summer-house in the background, another in the foreground. Enter the Duke and Lorenzo, wrapped in their mantles; Giomo, carrying a lantern.)

THE DUKE. If she keeps us waiting another quarter of an hour, I shall go. It is as cold as Greenland.

LORENZO. Be patient, my lord, be patient!

THE DUKE. She was to leave her mother's at midnight; it is midnight now, and yet she does not come.

LORENZO. If she does not come, say that I am a fool, and that the old mother is a virtuous woman.

THE DUKE. Good heavens; I dare say I am robbed of a thousand ducats.

LORENZO. We advanced only half. I will answer for the girl. One is never deceived by two great languishing eyes like that. What is more interesting for a connoisseur than the seduction of innocence? To behold in a child of fifteen the courtesan of the future, to study, to sow, to weave the mysterious thread of vice into a friendly council, a caress of the chin, to say everything in nothing, according to the degree of intimacy, to gently accustom the developing imagination to give form to its phantoms, to draw near to that which affrights, to scorn that which protects, is easier than you think! The important thing is to begin rightly. And what a treasure this one is! All that is needful to give your lordship a delicious night! So much modesty! A kitten that wishes for preserves, but does not wish to soil its paws! Neat as a Flemish maid! Middle-class mediocrity personified. In addition to which, daughter of honest people, whose slender means prevented their giving her a solid education; no depth to their principles, only a superficial polish; but what a strong surge of a noble river beneath that fragile film of ice which cracks at every step! Never did blooming bush produce fruit more rare; never did I inhale in childlike atmosphere a more exquisite odor of the courtier's art.

THE DUKE. Confound it! I see no signs of her. I must go to the Nasi's ball, however; it is to-day that he marries his daughter.

GIOMO. Let us go to the pavilion, my lord; since it is only a question of carrying off a girl who is half paid for, we can surely tap upon the window.

THE DUKE. Come along! The Hungarian is right.

(Exeunt. Enter Maffio.)

MAFFIO. It seems to me, in my dream, that I saw my sister cross our garden, carrying a dark-lantern, and covered with jewels. I awoke with a start. God knows that it was only an illusion, but an illusion too vivid to prevent sleep from flying before it. Thank Heaven, the windows of the pavilion where she sleeps are closed as usual! I see dimly the light of her lamp between the leaves of our old fig-tree. Now my foolish fears are dispersing; the palpitation of my heart gives place to a sweet tranquility. Fool that I am, my eyes are filled with tears, as if my poor sister had encountered some real danger.... What do I hear? What is moving there between the branches?

(The sister of Maffio passes in the distance.)

MAFFIO. Am I awake? It is the phantom of my sister! It is carrying a dark-lantern, and a necklace of brilliants is sparkling upon its breast, in the rays of the moonlight. Gabrielle! Gabrielle! Where are you going?

(Re-enter the Duke and Giomo.)

GIOMO. That must be her simpleton of a brother walking in his sleep. Lorenzo will escort your beauty to the palace by way of the small gate; and as for us, what have we to fear?

MAFFIO. Who are you? Hallo! Stop! *(He draws his sword.)*

GIOMO. We are your friends, clown.

MAFFIO. Where is my sister? What are you looking for here?

GIOMO. Your sister has run away, bold rascal! Open your garden gate.

MAFFIO. Draw your sword and defend yourself, assassin that you are!

(Giomo springs upon him and disarms him.)

GIOMO. Stop that, you big fool; not so fast!

MAFFIO. Oh, shame! Oh, excess of calamity! If there are any laws in Florence, if justice still lives upon earth, by all that is good and holy in the world, I will throw myself at the feet of the Duke, and he will have you both hanged.

GIOMO. At the feet of the Duke?

MAFFIO. Yes, yes, I know that scoundrels like you ruin families with impunity. But if I die, you understand, I shall not die in silence, as so many others have done. If the Duke does not know that his city is a forest full of bandits, full of poisoners and dishonored women, here is one who will tell it to him. Ah, butchery! ah, steel and blood! I will obtain justice of you!

GIOMO *(sword in hand)*. Shall I stab him, my lord?

THE DUKE. Nonsense! Stab this poor man? Go to bed, my friend; we will send you some ducats to-morrow. *(Exit Duke.)*

MAFFIO. It is Alexander de Medicis!

GIOMO. Himself, my bold rascal! Do not boast of his visit if you value your ears. *(Exit Giomo.)*

SCENE II

(A street. Sunrise. Several masqueraders come out of a lighted mansion. A Mercer and a Goldsmith opening their shops.)

THE MERCER. Ah, ah! Father Mondella, too much wind for my wares. *(He spreads out his pieces of silk.)*

THE GOLDSMITH *(yawning)*. This is enough to split a body's head. The devil take their ball! I did not sleep a wink all night.

THE MERCER. Neither did my wife, neighbor; the poor soul twisted and turned like an eel. But, bless me! a body doesn't sleep at the sound of violins when a body is young.

THE GOLDSMITH. Young! young! It pleases you to say that. A body it not young with a beard like this; and, moreover, God knows their damned music does not give me any desire to dance!

(Two students pass.)

FIRST STUDENT. Nothing is more amusing. We will step in near the door, among the soldiers, and see them come down the steps in their costumes of all colors. Come on! This is the Nasi house. *(He blows upon his fingers.)* My portfolio is freezing my fingers.

SECOND STUDENT. Will they allow us to come near?

FIRST STUDENT. By what right would they prevent us from doing so? We are citizens of Florence. Look at all those people around the door; look at the horses, the pages, and the liveries! They all go and come; it is only necessary to be slightly acquainted here. I can call all of the important people by name. You observe the costumes closely, and say at the studio in the evening: "I am very sleepy; I spent last night at the ball at Prince Aldobrandini's, or at Count Salviati's; the Prince wore such and such a costume; the Princess such another," and you tell no lie. Come along; take hold of the back of my cape.

(They place themselves near the door of the house.)

THE GOLDSMITH. Did you hear those young idlers? I should like to have one of my apprentices play such a trick as that!

THE MERCER. Nonsense! nonsense! Father Mondella, where pleasure costs nothing, youth has nothing to lose. The great wondering eyes of these young blackguards cheer up my heart. That is how I used to be, sniffing the air and seeking to know what was going on. It seems that the Nasi girl is a lively beauty, and that young Martelli is a fortunate lad. A true Florentine family, that! What a figure all these great personages cut! I confess that such entertainments please me. You lie comfortably in bed, with a corner of the curtain drawn back; you see the lights flitting about the palace from time to time; you pick up a little air of dance music for nothing, and you say to yourself: "Ah, ha! those are my goods that are dancing, my beautiful goods of the good God, upon the dear backs of all those brave and loyal noblemen."

THE GOLDSMITH. There is more than one dancing who has not paid for what he wears, neighbor; those are the ones that a body would willingly duck into the water, or butt against a wall. It is quite natural that the grandees should amuse themselves they were born for that; but there are various kinds of amusement, you understand.

THE MERCER. Yes, yes, such as dancing, horseback riding, tennis, and many more. What do you mean by that, Father Mondella?

THE GOLDSMITH. Enough said. I know what I mean. It is that the walls of all these palaces have never better proven their solidity. They needed less strength to protect the ancestors against water from the clouds, than they need to sustain the sons when they are far gone in their cups.

THE MERCER. A glass of wine is a good counselor, Father Mondella. Come into my shop while I show you a piece of velvet.

THE GOLDSMITH. Yes, a good ,counselor, and looks well, neighbor; a good glass of old wine looks well in a hand that has toiled for it; one tosses it off cheerfully at a single swallow, and it encourages the heart of an honest man who works for his family. But all these coxcombs at court are shameless sots. Whom does a man please when he gets beastly drunk? Nobody, not even himself, and still less his Creator.

THE MERCER. The carnival was rough, it must be confessed; and their cursed balloon spoiled fifty florins worth of merchandise for me! Thank God! the Strozzis paid for it.

THE GOLDSMITH. The Strozzis! May Heaven confound those who dared to raise a hand against their nephew! Philippe Strozzi is the bravest man in Florence.

THE MERCER. That did not prevent Pierre Strozzi from dragging his cursed balloon across my shop, and making three large spots in a piece of embroidered velvet for me. By the way, Father Mondella, shall we meet at Mount Olivet?

THE GOLDSMITH. It is not my business to follow fairs; I shall go to Mount Olivet, however, as an act of piety. It is a holy pilgrimage, neighbor, and one that makes remission of all sins.

THE MERCER. And one which is altogether time-honored, neighbor, and merchants make more than on all other days of the year. It is a pleasure to see the good dames, as they come from mass, stop to handle and examine all the goods. God preserve his lordship! The court is a fine thing.

THE GOLDSMITH. The court! The people carry it upon their backs. Florence was once not so very long ago a good house well built; all the fine palaces which are the lodgings of our great families were its pillars. There was not one of all those pillars that exceeded the others by a hair's breadth; together they sustained an ancient arch, well cemented, and we walked beneath it without fear of a stone falling upon our heads. But there are two ill-advised architects in the world who have ruined the structure. I say this to you in confidence; they are the Pope and the Emperor Charles. The Emperor began by entering the aforesaid house through a tolerably large breach. After that they judged it proper to take one of the pillars of which I speak namely, that of the Medicis family and make of it a steeple, which steeple sprang up like a mushroom of misfortune in the space of a single night, and then, do you know, neighbor, as the edifice swayed to the wind, since it was top-heavy and minus a limb, they replaced the pillar which had been turned into a steeple, by a great formless block made of mud and spittle, and that they called the citadel. The Germans have installed themselves in that accursed hole, like rats in a cheese; and it is a fine thing to know, that while they are playing dice and drinking their sour wine, they have an eye upon the rest of us. The Florentine families have well complained, and the people and merchants have well said, that the Medicis govern by means of their garrison; they devour us as a malignant ulcer devours a diseased stomach. It is by virtue of halberdiers who promenade the ramparts, that a bastard, who is but half a Medicis, a blockhead that Heaven created for a butcher's boy or a plowman, corrupts our daughters, drinks our wine, and smashes our windows; still the people pay him for it.

THE MERCER. Dear me! dear me! How you go on! You appear to know all that by heart. It would not be wise to say that to every ear, neighbor Mondella.

THE GOLDSMITH. Even if they should banish me like so many others, one can live at Rome as well as here. The devil take their ball; those who are dancing at it and those who give it. *(He goes in.)*

(The Mercer mingles with the curious. A citizen passes with his wife.)

THE WIFE. Guillaume Martelli is a handsome man and a rich one. Nicolo Nasi is fortunate to have a son-in-law like that. Bless me! the ball is going on yet. Look at all those lights!

THE CITIZEN. And how about our daughter; when will we marry her?

THE WIFE. How everything is lighted up! To be dancing yet, at this time of day, it must be a beautiful ball! They say the Duke is there.

THE CITIZEN. To turn day into night and night into day is a convenient method of creating rogues. A fine invention, indeed. Halberdiers at the door of a wedding! God protect the city! Something new every day, with those German curs, from their damned fortress.

THE WIFE. Look at that pretty mask! Ah, what a beautiful gown! Alas! that all costs a great deal of money, and we are very poor at our house.

(Exeunt.)

A SOLDIER *(to the Mercer).* Out of the way, scoundrel! Let the horses pass.

THE MERCER. Scoundrel yourself, you devilish German!

(The soldier strikes him with his pike.)

THE MERCER *(falling back)*. This is the way they follow up the capitulation! These blackguards abuse the citizens. *(He goes into his shop.)*

THE STUDENT *(to his comrade)*. Do you see that one who is taking off his mask? That is Palla Ruccellai a haughty fellow! The short man beside him is Thomas Strozzi—Masaccio, as they call him.

A PAGE *(calling)*. His lordship's horse!

SECOND STUDENT. Let us be off; there comes the Duke.

FIRST STUDENT. Are you afraid that he will eat you?

(The crowd increases before the door.)

FIRST STUDENT. That is Nicolini; and that one is the purveyor.

(The Duke comes out, dressed like a nun, with Julien Salviati dressed the same, both masked.)

THE DUKE *(mounting his horse)*. Are you coming, Julien?

SALVIATI. No, not yet, my lord. *(He whispers in his ear.)*

THE DUKE. Well, well, cheer up!

SALVIATI. She is as beautiful as a demon. Leave everything to me; if I can get rid of my wife... *(He returns to the ball.)*

THE DUKE. You are drunk, Salviati; the devil take me, you are staggering! *(He goes off with his suite.)*

THE STUDENT. It will soon be over, now that the Duke has left.

(The masqueraders go off in all directions.)

SECOND STUDENT. Red, green, blue my eyes are dazzled, my head swims.

A CITIZEN. It seems that the supper lasted a long time; there are two who can not stand straight.

(The purveyor mounts his horse; a broken bottle falls on his shoulder.)

THE PURVEYOR. What the deuce! Who did that?

A MASKER. Ah, do you not see him, Lord Corsini! There! look at that window; it is Lorenzo in his nun's robe.

THE PURVEYOR. Lorenzaccio, the devil take you! You have wounded my horse.

(The window is closed.)

11

THE PURVEYOR. Plague take the drunkard and his sly tricks! A blackguard who never smiled three times in his life, and who spends his time in playing the pranks of a schoolboy! *(Exit.)*

(Louise Strozzi comes out of the house, accompanied by Julie Salviati; he holds her stirrup. She mounts her horse; a groom and a governess follow her.)

SALVIATI. A pretty leg, dear girl! You are a sunbeam which has penetrated to my very marrow.

LOUISE. That is not the language of a gentleman, my lord.

SALVIATI. What eyes you have, dear heart! What a beautiful shoulder to dry, all moist and fresh! What would I not give to be your waiting-maid this night... to bare this pretty foot!

LOUISE. Let go of my foot, Salviati!

SALVIATI. No, by Bacchus! Not until you have given me a rendezvous.

(Louise strikes her horse and goes off at a gallop.)

A MASKER *(to Salviati).* The fair Mademoiselle Strozzi is going away, as red as fire. You have offended her, Salviati.

SALVIATI. Pshaw! A girl's anger and a morning shower... *(Exit.)*

SCENE III

(The Marquis of Cibo's House. The Marquis, in traveling costume, the Marquise, Ascanio, Cardinal Cibo, seated.)

THE MARQUIS *(kissing his little boy).* I wish that I could take you, darling, you and that great sword which you are riding. Be a good boy; Massa is not very far, and I will bring you a nice present.

THE MARQUISE. Good-by, Laurent. Come back—come back soon!

THE CARDINAL. Marquise, you weep too much. Would not a body say that my brother was setting out for Palestine? He runs no great danger upon his estates, I think.

THE MARQUIS. Speak no evil of these beautiful tears, brother.

(He kisses his wife.)

THE CARDINAL. I could only wish that virtue had not that appearance.

THE MARQUISE. Has virtue no tears, sir Cardinal? Are they all for repentance and fear?

THE MARQUIS. No, by heavens! for the best of them are for love. Dry not these upon my cheek; the wind will do that upon the way. May they dry slowly! Well, my dear, have you no message for your favorites? Am I not to carry, as usual, some fine, sentimental speech, to deliver for you to the rocks and rills of my old patrimony?

THE MARQUISE. Ah, my poor little cascades!

THE MARQUIS. That is true, sweetheart; they are all sad without you. *(He lowers his voice.)* They used to be joyous, did they not, Ricciarda?

THE MARQUISE. Take me with you!

THE MARQUIS. I would do so were I mad, and I am almost, with all my warlike front. Let us say no more about it; it will only be for a week. Let my dear Ricciarda see her gardens when they are quiet and peaceful; the muddy feet of my farmers shall leave no trace in those beloved alleys. It is for me to count my old tree-trunks which remind me of your Father Alberic, and all the blades of grass of my woodland; the tenants and their herds, all that is my affair. With the first flower that I shall see growing I will set everything aside, and then I will take you.

THE MARQUISE. The first flower of our beautiful lawn is always dear to me. The winter is so long! It always seems to me that the poor little things will never come again.

ASCANIO. What horse are you going to ride, father?

THE MARQUIS. Come with me to the courtyard and you shall see.

(Exeunt. The Marquise remains alone with the Cardinal. A silence.)

THE CARDINAL. Did you not ask me to hear your confession to-day, Marquise?

THE MARQUISE. Dispense me from it, Cardinal. It shall be for this evening, if your Eminence is at liberty, or to-morrow, as you please. I have not time just now.

(She goes to the window and signals farewell to her husband.)

THE CARDINAL. If regrets were permitted to a faithful servant of the Lord, I should envy the lot of my brother. So short a journey, so simple, so peaceful! A visit to one of his estates which is but a few paces from here! An absence of a week, and so much sorrow, such sweet sorrow, may I say, at his departure! Happy is he who knows how to make himself so beloved after seven years of marriage! Is it not seven years, Marquise?

THE MARQUISE. Yes, Cardinal; my son is six years old.

THE CARDINAL. Were you at the wedding at the Nasi's last evening?

THE MARQUISE. Yes, I was there.

THE CARDINAL. And the Duke, dressed as a nun?

THE MARQUISE. Why the Duke dressed as a nun?

THE CARDINAL. I was told that he had taken that costume; it may be that I was misinformed.

THE MARQUISE. He did take it, in fact. Ah, Malaspina, these are sorry times for all sacred things!

THE CARDINAL. A person can respect sacred things, and, on a day of frolic, take the costume of certain convents, without any hostile intention toward the Holy Catholic Church.

THE MARQUISE. The example is to be feared, and not the intention. I do not agree with you; that was revolting to me. It is true that I do not know very well what one may or may not do, according to your mysterious rules. God knows where they lead! Those who place words upon an anvil and distort them with hammer and file do not always reflect that words represent thoughts, and thoughts actions.

THE CARDINAL. Well, well! The Duke is young, Marquise, and I wager that that bewitching nun's costume was marvelously becoming to him.

THE MARQUISE. Nothing could have been more so; it lacked only a few drops of the blood of his cousin, Hippolyte de Medicis.

THE CARDINAL. And the liberty cap, is it not true, dear sister? What hatred for the poor Duke!

THE MARQUISE. And you, his right hand, it is all the same to you that the Duke of Florence is the prefect of Charles V, the civil commissioner of the Pope, as Baccio is his religious commissioner? It is all the same to you, the brother of my Laurent, that our sun casts German shadows upon the citadel, that Caesar speaks here in every mouth, that debauchery serves as a procuress to slavery, and shakes its bells above the sobs of the people? Ah! the clergy would ring all the bells at need, to drown the noise of it and to awaken the imperial eagle, if he were sleeping upon our roofs. *(Exit Marquise.)*

THE CARDINAL *(alone, raises the portière and calls in a low voice).* Agnolo!

(Enter a page.)

THE CARDINAL. What is there new to-day?

AGNOLO. This letter, my lord.

THE CARDINAL. Give it to me.

AGNOLO. Alas! my lord, it is a sin.

THE CARDINAL. Nothing is a sin when one obeys a priest of the Roman Church.

(Agnolo hands him the letter.)

THE CARDINAL. It is amusing to listen to the anger of that poor Marquise, and to see her running to a rendezvous with the dear tyrant, all bathed in republican tears. *(He opens the letter and reads.)* "Either you will be mine, or you will have been the means of my misfortune, your own, and that of our two houses." The Duke's style is laconic, but it does not lack force. Whether the Marquise will be convinced or not, it is difficult to tell. Two months of almost diligent love-making is much for Alexander; it ought to be enough for Ricciarda Cibo. *(He returns the letter to the page.)* Carry that to your mistress; you are always silent, are you not?

AGNOLO. Rely upon me.

(He gives him his hand to kiss and goes off.)

SCENE IV

(A courtyard of the ducal palace. Duke Alexander upon a terrace; pages exercising horses in the courtyard. Enter Valori and Sir Maurice.)

THE DUKE. Has your Eminence received any news this morning from the court of Rome?

VALORI. Paul III sends a thousand blessings to your Lordship, and prays most earnestly for your prosperity.

THE DUKE. Only prayers, Valori?

VALORI. His Holiness fears that the Duke will create new dangers for himself by too many indulgences. The people are not accustomed to absolute government, and the Emperor, at his last visit, said as much, I think, to your Lordship.

THE DUKE. That is a fine horse, Sir Maurice! Ah, what a devilishly fine croup!

SIR MAURICE. Superb, my Lord.

THE DUKE. So, sir Apostolical Commissioner, there are still a few bad branches to be chopped off. Caesar and the Pope created me a king; but, by Bacchus, they have put into my hand a species of scepter which scents the ax for a league. Well, let us see, Valori, what is it?

VALORI. I am a priest, my Lord; if the words which my duty compels me to report faithfully to you have been interpreted in a manner so severe, my heart forbids me to add one word to them.

THE DUKE. Yes, yes, I know you for a valiant man. You are, by Heaven, the only honest priest that I have even seen in my life!

VALORI. My Lord, honesty is the best policy under any guise; and among men there are more good than bad ones.

THE DUKE. And so no explanations?

SIR MAURICE. Do you wish me to speak, my Lord? Everything is easily explained.

THE DUKE. Well, Sir Maurice.

SIR MAURICE. The licentiousness of the court irritates the Pope.

THE DUKE. What is that you say, sir?

SIR MAURICE. I said the licentiousness of the court, my Lord; the actions of the Duke have no other judge than himself. It is Lorenzo de Medicis that the Pope reclaims as a fugitive from his justice.

THE DUKE. From his justice? He has never offended a pope, to my knowledge, excepting Clement VII, my late cousin, who at this hour is in hell.

SIR MAURICE. Clement VII allowed to leave his domain a libertine who in a day of drunkenness had mutilated the statues of the Arch of Constantine. Paul III can never forgive that titled model of Florentine debauchery.

THE DUKE. Zounds! Alexander Farnese is a ridiculous fellow! If debauchery shocks him, what the devil does he do with his bastard, the dear Pierre Farnese, who treats the Bishop of Fano so prettily? That mutilation is always being raked up against poor Renzo. I think it a joke, myself, to have cut off the heads of all those men of stone. I protect art as well as another, and I have at my court the best artists in Italy, but I can not understand the regard of the Pope for those statues which he would excommunicate to-morrow if they were flesh and blood.

SIR MAURICE. Lorenzo is an atheist; he scoffs at everything. If the government of your Lordship be not surrounded with a profound respect it can not be strong. The people call Lorenzo, Lorenzaccio; they know that he directs your pleasures, and that is enough.

THE DUKE. Peace! you forget that Lorenzo de Medicis is cousin to Alexander.

(Enter Cardinal Cibo.)

THE DUKE. Cardinal, listen to these gentlemen, who say that the Pope is scandalized by the disorders of poor Renzo, and contend that they are weakening my government.

THE CARDINAL. Chancellor Francesco Nolza has just delivered at the Roman Academy an harangue in Latin against the mutilation of the Arch of Constantine.

THE DUKE. Nonsense—you make me mad! Renzo, a man to fear! The most arrant coward! An effeminate man, the shadow of a nerveless ruffian! A dreamer who never carries a sword for fear of seeing its shadow at his side! In addition to which, a philosopher, a scribbler, a bad poet who can not even compose a sonnet! No, no; I am not yet afraid of phantoms. Ah, body of Bacchus! what do I care for Latin speeches and the quibbles of my rabble! I like Lorenzo, and, by the Lord! he shall remain here.

THE CARDINAL. If I were afraid of that man, it would not be for your court, nor for Florence, but for you, Duke.

THE DUKE. Are you joking, Cardinal, and do you wish me to tell you the truth? *(He lowers his voice.)* All that I know of these damned exiles, of all these headstrong republicans who are plotting around me, I know through Lorenzo. He is as slippery as an eel; he forces his way everywhere and tells me everything. Did he not find means of establishing a correspondence with all those infernal Strozzis? Yes, certainly, he is my intermediator; but believe that his intervention, if it injures any one, will not injure me. There!

(Lorenzo appears at the back of a low balcony.)

THE DUKE. Look at that slender frame this day after a strolling orgy. Look at those heavy eyes, those skinny hands, scarce strong enough to wield a fan; that dull face, which sometimes smiles, but has not the force to laugh. Is that a man to fear? Come, come! you are making fun of him. Hey, Renzo! come here; here is Sir Maurice, who is seeking a quarrel with you.

LORENZO *(mounting the steps of the terrace).* Good morning, gentlemen, friends of my cousin!

THE DUKE. Lorenzo, listen here. We have been talking of you for an hour. Do you know the news? My friend, you are excommunicated in Latin, and Sir Maurice calls you a dangerous man, the Cardinal also; as for honest Valori, he is too virtuous to pronounce your name.

LORENZO. Dangerous for whom, your Eminence—for women of pleasure, or saints of Paradise?

THE CARDINAL. Dogs at court can be seized with madness like other dogs.

LORENZO. A priestly insult should be given in Latin.

SIR MAURICE. It is given in Tuscan, to which you can reply.

LORENZO. Sir Maurice, I did not see you; excuse me, the sun was in my eyes; but you look well, and your coat seems to me quite new.

SIR MAURICE. Like your wit. I had it made out of my grandfather's old doublet.

LORENZO. Cousin, when you are tired of some conquest of the suburbs, send her to Sir Maurice. It is not good for a man with a short neck and hairy hands, like him, to lead a life of continence.

SIR MAURICE. He who thinks he has the right to joke should know how to defend himself. If I were in your place I would draw my sword.

LORENZO. If anybody told you that I was a Soldier, it was a mistake; I am only a poor lover of science.

SIR MAURICE. Your wit is a keen sword, but flexible. It is too vile a weapon; each one makes use of his own. *(He draws his sword.)*

VALORI. Before the Duke, the bare sword!

THE DUKE *(laughing)*. Let them alone—let them alone. Come, Renzo, I want to serve you as a second; somebody give him a sword!

LORENZO. My Lord, what are you saying?

THE DUKE. Ah, well! Do your spirits fade so quickly? You tremble, cousin? For shame! you dishonor the name of Medicis. I am only a bastard, but I bear it better than you, who are legitimate. A sword! a sword! A Medicis does not allow himself to be challenged thus. Pages, come up here; all the court shall see it, and I wish that all Florence were here.

LORENZO. Your Lordship is laughing at me!

THE DUKE. I was laughing a moment ago, but now I am blushing with shame. A sword!

(He takes a sword from a page and presents it to Lorenzo.)

VALORI. My Lord, this is carrying the thing too far. A sword drawn in the presence of your Lordship is a crime punishable within the palace.

THE DUKE. Who speaks here while I am speaking?

VALORI. Your Lordship could have had no other design than that of amusing yourself for a moment, and Sir Maurice himself was actuated by no other thought.

THE DUKE. And you do not see that I am joking still! Who the devil thinks of a serious affair? Look at Renzo, if you please: his knees are trembling; he would have turned pale, if he could. Good heavens, what an expression! I believe he is going to faint.

(Lorenzo totters; he leans upon the balustrade and sinks suddenly to the ground.)

THE DUKE *(laughing aloud).* I told you so! No one knows better than I; the very sight of a sword makes him ill. Come, dear little Lorenzo, you must be taken to your mother.

(The pages carry Lorenzo off.)

SIR MAURICE. Doubly a coward! Son of a harlot!

THE DUKE. Silence, Sir Maurice! Weigh your words, I tell you; no such speeches as that in my presence.

(Exit Sir Maurice.)

VALORI. Poor young man! *(Exit.)*

THE CARDINAL *(alone with the Duke).* Do you believe that, my Lord?

THE DUKE. I wish I knew some reason for not believing it.

THE CARDINAL. Hum! it is incredible.

THE DUKE. That is just the reason I believe it. Do you imagine that a Medicis would disgrace himself publicly for the pleasure of it? Furthermore, it is not the first time that that has happened to him; he never could bear the sight of a sword.

THE CARDINAL. It is incredible! It is incredible!

(Exeunt.)

SCENE V

(Before the Church of Saint Miniato at Mount Olivet. The congregation coming out of the church.)

A WOMAN *(to her neighbor).* Do you return to Florence this evening?

19

THE NEIGHBOR. I never stay here more than an hour, and I never come but one Friday; I can not afford to stay at the fair. I only come to make my devotions, and if that suffices for my salvation, that is all that I need.

A LADY OF THE COURT *(to another)*. How well he preached! He is my daughter's confessor. *(They approach a shop.)* White and gold, that does well enough for evening, but how can you keep clean in it during the day?

(The Mercer and the Goldsmith before their shops with some cavaliers.)

THE GOLDSMITH. The citadel! That is what the people will never stand, to see suddenly arise over the city, this new Tower of Babel, in the midst of the most accursed gibberish; the Germans will never thrive in Florence, and it would require a vigorous hand to implant them there.

THE MERCER. Come in, ladies. Will your ladyships take a seat in my booth?

A CAVALIER. You are of old Florentine blood, Father Mondella; the hatred of tyranny still makes your wrinkled fingers tremble over the precious sculptures at the back of your shop.

THE GOLDSMITH. That is true, my Lord. If I were a great artist, I should like princes, because they alone can undertake great works! Great artists have no country; I only make holy pyxes and sword-hilts.

ANOTHER CAVALIER. Apropos of an artist. Do you not see, in that little ale-house, that great big fellow gesticulating before the idlers? He is striking his glass upon the table. If I am not mistaken, it is that braggart of a Cellini.

THE FIRST CAVALIER. Let us go over there, then; with a glass of wine aboard, it is amusing to hear him, and probably he is telling some good yarn.

(Exeunt. Two citizens take seats.)

FIRST CITIZEN. Has there been a riot at Florence?

SECOND CITIZEN. Scarcely anything. A few poor young men were killed in the old marketplace.

FIRST CITIZEN. What a pity for their families!

SECOND CITIZEN. These are inevitable misfortunes. What would you have the youth of a government like ours do? Somebody announces with the sound of a trumpet that Caesar is at Bologna, and the idlers repeat, "Caesar is at Bologna!" and wink with an air of importance, without reflecting what they are doing. The next day they are happier still to learn and to repeat, "The Pope is at Bologna with Caesar!" What follows? A public rejoicing they see nothing more in it; and then some fine morning they awaken all stupefied with the fumes of imperial wine, and they see a sinister face at the great window of the Pazzi palace. They demand who the personage is; they are told it is the King. The Pope and the Emperor are delivered of a bastard who has the right of life and death over our children, and who can not call his own mother by name.

THE GOLDSMITH *(drawing near)*. You talk like a patriot, my friend. I advise you to look out for that lanky fellow.

(A German officer appears.)

THE OFFICER. Get off of there, gentlemen; some ladies wish to sit down.

(Two ladies of the court enter and take the seats.)

FIRST LADY. Is that from Venice?
THE MERCER. Yes, your Ladyship; shall I cut you a few yards of it?
FIRST LADY. If you please. I thought I saw Julien Salviati pass.
THE OFFICER. He promenades before the door of the church. He is a gallant.
SECOND LADY. He is an insolent fellow! Show me some silk stockings.
THE OFFICER. There will not be any small enough for you.
FIRST LADY. Nonsense! you must always talk. Since you see Julien, go and tell him that I wish to speak to him.
THE OFFICER. I will go and fetch him. *(Exit.)*
FIRST LADY. What a fool your officer is! What can you make of him?
SECOND LADY. You will know that there is nothing better than that man.

(They withdraw to the background. Enter the Prior of Capua.)

THE PRIOR. Give me a glass of lemonade, good man. *(He sits down.)*
ONE OF THE CITIZENS. That is the Prior of Capua. There is a patriot for you!

(The two citizens sit down again.)

THE PRIOR. You come from the church, gentlemen. What did you think of the sermon?

THE CITIZEN. It was beautiful, M. Prior.

SECOND CITIZEN *(to the Goldsmith)*. The nobleness of the Strozzi is dear to the people, because it is not vain. Is it not a pleasure to see a fine gentleman talk freely and affably to his neighbors? It does one more good than you think.

THE PRIOR. To speak frankly, I found the sermon too fine. I have preached sometimes, and I have never extracted any great glory from the rattling of windows; but a little tear upon the cheek of a brave man has always been to me a great prize.

(Enter Salviati.)

SALVIATI. I was told that there were some ladies here who asked for me just now; but I see no gown here but yours, Prior. Am I mistaken?

THE MERCER. You were correctly informed, sir. They have gone away; but I think that they will return. Here are ten yards of goods and four pairs of stockings for them.

SALVIATI *(sitting down)*. That is a pretty woman who is passing. Where the devil have I seen her? Ah, zounds! it was in my bed.

THE PRIOR *(to the citizen)*. I think I saw your signature upon a letter addressed to the Duke.

THE CITIZEN. I proclaim it aloud; it was the petition offered up by the exiles.

THE PRIOR. Have you any in your family?

THE CITIZEN. Two, your excellency: my father and my uncle. There is no man but I at the house now.

SECOND CITIZEN *(to the Goldsmith)*. What a vile tongue that Salviati has!

THE GOLDSMITH. That is not astonishing: a man half-ruined, living upon the generosity of the Medicis, and married, as he is, to a woman who is dishonored everywhere! He would like to have people say of as many wives as possible what they say of his.

SALVIATI. Is not that Louise Strozzi who is passing yonder on the hillside?

THE MERCER. 'Tis she, my Lord. Few women of our nobility are unknown to me. If I am not mistaken, that is her younger sister that she is leading by the hand.

SALVIATI. I met that Louise last night at the Nasi's ball. Upon my word, she has a pretty leg, and she is to give me a rendezvous at the first opportunity.

THE PRIOR *(turning around).* What do you mean by that?

SALVIATI. That is very plain; she told me so herself. I was holding her stirrup, scarcely thinking of malice; I do not know by what abstraction I seized her leg, and that is how it all came about.

THE PRIOR. Julien, I do not know whether you are aware that it is my sister that you are talking about, or not.

SALVIATI. I know it very well. All women are made for man's pleasure, and your sister can well be for mine.

THE PRIOR *(arising).* Do I owe you something, my good man? *(He throws a piece of money on the table and goes out.)*

SALVIATI. I like that good prior very much, whom an insult to his sister makes forget his change. Would you not think that all the virtue in Florence was concentrated in that Strozzi family? See there he is turning around. Frown as much as you like, you will not frighten me. *(Exit.)*

SCENE VI

(A bank of the Arno. Marie Soderini, Catherine.)

CATHERINE. The sun is setting. Large bands of purple strike athwart the foliage, and the frog is ringing his little crystal bell beneath the rushes. A singular thing is this harmony of evening with the distant sound of that city.

MARIE. It is time to go in; tie your veil around your neck.

CATHERINE. Not yet, at least if you are not cold. Look, my dear mother, how beautiful the sky is! how vast and tranquil! How God is everywhere! But you lower your head; you are anxious since this morning.

MARIE. Not anxious, but distressed. Did you not hear that fatal story of Lorenzo repeated? He is the laughing-stock of Florence.

CATHERINE. O mother! Cowardice is not a crime; courage is not a virtue; why is weakness blamable? To respond to the beatings of his heart is a sad privilege; God alone can make him noble, and worthy of admiration. And why should not that child have the right that we all have, we women? A woman who is not afraid of anything is not worthy of being loved, they say.

MARIE. Would you love a man who is a coward? You blush, Catherine. Lorenzo is your nephew; you can not love him; but imagine if he were called by another name, what would you think of him? What woman would wish to lean upon his arm to mount her horse? What man would grasp his hand?

CATHERINE. That is sad, and yet it is not for that he is most to be pitied. His heart is perhaps not that of a Medicis; but, alas! it is still less that of an honest man.

MARIE. Let us talk no more about it, Catherine; it is painful enough for a mother not to be able to talk about her son.

CATHERINE. Ah, that Florence! That was his ruin. Have I not sometimes seen the fire of a noble ambition burning in his eyes? Did not his youth give promise of a brilliant future? And often, even now, it seems to me that a sudden spark... I say in spite of myself that all is not dead within him.

MARIE. Ah, it is all so unfathomable! Such a facility of conception, such a sweet love for solitude! He will never be a warrior, my Renzo, I used to say to myself on seeing him come in from school, dripping with perspiration, with his books under his arm; and such a holy love of truth burned upon his lips and in his black eyes! He was so solicitous about everybody, constantly saying, "So-and-so is poor," or " So-and-so is ruined; what can we do for them?" And that admiration for the great men of his Plutarch! Catherine, Catherine, how often I used to kiss his brow in thinking of the father of the country!

CATHERINE. Do not grieve so, mother.

MARIE. I say that I do wish to speak of him, and yet I talk of him incessantly. There are some things, you know, that mothers never cease to talk about as long as they live. If my son had been a vulgar debauchee, if the strain of Soderini blood in his veins had been less strong, I should not despair; but I had hopes, and I had reason for having them. Ah, Catherine, he is no longer even handsome; like a noxious vapor, the defilement of his heart has mounted to his face. The smile, that gentle expansion of countenance which makes youth like unto flowers, has fled from his sallow cheeks, to leave imprinted there an ignoble irony and a contempt of everything.

CATHERINE. He is still handsome sometimes, with his strange melancholy.

MARIE. Did not his birth entitle him to a throne? Would he not have been able some day to take with him there the science of a doctor, the fairest mistress in the world, and so crown all my cherished dreams with a diadem of gold? Did I not have reason to expect that? Ah, Catherine, in order to sleep peacefully, one should not have had certain dreams. It is too cruel to have lived in a fairy castle, where angels' songs were murmuring, to have slept there, cradled by one's son, and then to awaken in a blood-stained hovel filled with the remains of revelry and dead men's bones, in the arms of a hideous specter which stabs you to the heart, in calling you still by the sacred name of mother!

CATHERINE. The silent shadows are beginning to creep across the path; let us go in, Marie. I am afraid of all these exiles.

MARIE. Poor men! They ought only to inspire pity. Ah, can I no longer see a single thing that does not pierce me to the heart? Must I never open my eyes again? Alas, my Cattina! this again is Lorenzo's work. All these poor people had confidence in him; there is not one among all these fathers driven from their homes that my son has not betrayed. Thus has he turned to infamous use even the glorious memory of his ancestors. The republicans appeal to him as the scion of their old protector; his house is open to them; the Strozzis themselves come there. Poor Philippe! His gray hairs will go down in sorrow to the grave. Ah, can I not see a shameless girl, an unfortunate deprived of his family, without they cry to me, "You are the mother of our misfortunes!" When shall I be there? *(She strikes the ground.)*

CATHERINE. My poor mother, your tears are contagious.

(They depart. The sun has set. A group of exiles forms in the midst of the field.)

AN EXILE. Where are you going?

ANOTHER EXILE. To Pisa. And you?

THE FIRST EXILE. To Rome.

ANOTHER EXILE. And I to Venice. These two go to Ferrara. What will become of us, so widely separated from each other?

A FOURTH EXILE. Good-by, neighbor, until better times. *(He starts off.)* Good-by; you and I can go together as far as the Cross of the Virgin.

(Exit with another. Maffio arrives.)

THE FIRST EXILE. Is this you, Maffio? By what chance are you here?

MAFFIO. I am one of you. You know the Duke has carried off my sister. I drew my sword; a species of tiger with claws of steel threw himself upon my neck and disarmed me; after that I received a purse full of ducats and an order to leave the city.

THE SECOND EXILE. And where is your sister?

MAFFIO. She was pointed out to me this evening coming out of the theater in a robe fit for an empress—may God forgive her! An old woman accompanied her, who left three of her teeth at the entrance. Never in my life have I dealt a blow of the fist which gave me so much pleasure as that.

THE THIRD EXILE. May they all burst in their vile debauchery, and we will die content.

THE FOURTH EXILE. Philippe Strozzi will write to us at Venice. Some day we shall all be surprised to find an army at our command.

THE THIRD EXILE. Long live Philippe! As long as he has a hair in his head, Italian liberty is not dead.

(A part of the group detach themselves; all of the exiles embrace.)

A VOICE. Until better times!
ANOTHER VOICE. Until better times!

(Two exiles mount upon a platform from which the city can be seen.)

FIRST CITIZEN. Farewell, Florence, pest of Italy! Farewell, sterile mother who no longer has milk for her children!

SECOND CITIZEN. Farewell, Florence, vile city, hideous specter of your former greatness!

ALL THE EXILES. Farewell, Florence! Cursed be the breasts of your women! Cursed be your sobs! Cursed be the prayers of your churches, the bread of your harvests, the air of your streets! A curse upon the last drop of your corrupted blood!

ACT THE SECOND

SCENE I

(At the Strozzi Palace.)

PHILIPPE *(in his study)*. Ten citizens banished from this neighborhood alone! Old Galeazzo and young Maffio banished; his sister corrupted, become a prostitute in a single night! Poor girl! When will the education of the lower classes be such as to prevent young girls from laughing while their parents weep? Is corruption a law of nature? Is that which women call virtue but a Sunday frock which they put on to go to mass? The rest of the week they are at the window, and, as they knit, they watch the young men pass. Poor humanity! What name do you bear? That of birth, or that of baptism? And the rest of us old dreamers, what original spot have we washed out of the human face during the four or five thousand years that we have been mellowing with our books? How easy it is for you, in the stillness of your study, to trace, with a light hand, a line as clear and slender as a hair upon that white paper! How easy it is to build palaces and cities with that small compass and a little ink! But the architect who has thousands of admirable plans in his desk can not raise from the ground the first stone of his edifice, when he comes to set himself to the task with bent back and fixed determination. That the happiness of men is but a dream, that indeed is hard; that evil is irrevocable, eternal, impossible to change, no! Why does the philosopher who works for all things look about him? That is the mischief. The least speck which passes before his eyes blinds him to the light. Let us proceed more boldly. The Republic we need that word. And although it be but a word, it is something, since the people are aroused when they hear it... Ah, good morning, Leon!

(Enter the Prior of Capua.)

THE PRIOR. I have just come from the fair at Mount Olivet.

PHILIPPE. Was it fine? Here is Pierre also. Sit down; I want to talk to you.

THE PRIOR. It was very fine, and I had a rather pleasant time, excepting a little annoyance which still disturbs me.

PIERRE. Bah! what is it?

THE PRIOR. Imagine that I had gone into a shop to take a glass of lemonade... But no; what's the use? I'm a fool to think about it.

PHILIPPE. What the devil have you on your heart? You talk like a woman in distress.

THE PRIOR. It is no matter; an insult, nothing more. There is no importance to attach to it.

PIERRE. An insult? To whom? To yourself?

THE PRIOR. No, not exactly to myself. Little would I care for an insult to myself.

PIERRE. To whom, then? Come, speak, if you can.

THE PRIOR. I am wrong; a man does not remember such things as that when he knows the difference between a gentleman and a Salviati.

PIERRE. Salviati? What did that villain say?

THE PRIOR. He is a villain—you are righ—no matter what he said! A shameless man, a court lackey, who, according to all accounts, has a wife who is a most dissolute woman! Bah! The thing is past, I will think no more about it.

PIERRE. Think about it and speak about it, Léon. I long to take him by the ears. Whom did he slander? Us? Our father? Ah, blood of Christ! I do not waste any love upon that Salviati. I must know what he said, do you understand?

THE PRIOR. If you insist, I will tell you. He expressed himself before me, in a shop, in a truly offensive manner on the score of our sister.

PIERRE. Oh, my God! In what terms? Come, speak!

THE PRIOR. In the grossest terms.

PIERRE. Devil of a priest that you are! You see me beside myself with impatience, and you are choosing your words! Tell things as they are. Zounds! One word is as good as another; it is not to the good God that it pertains.

PHILIPPE. Pierre, Pierre! You are wanting in respect toward your brother.

THE PRIOR. He said that he was to have a rendezvous with—her that was his word—and that she had promised it to him.

PIERRE. That she had prom... Ah, death of death, of a thousand deaths! What time is it?

PHILIPPE. Where are you going? See here; you are too hot-headed. What are you going to do with that sword? You have one at your side.

PIERRE. I am not going to do anything with it. Let us go to dinner; dinner is ready.

(Exeunt.)

SCENE II

(The front of a church. Enter Lorenzo and Valori.)

VALORI. What is the reason that the Duke does not come? Ah, sir, what a satisfaction to a Christian is this magnificent pomp of the Roman Church! What man can be insensible to it? Should not an artist find there the Paradise of his heart? The warrior, the priest, and the merchant, do they not meet there all that they love! That admirable harmony of music, those splendid hangings of velvet and needlework, those paintings by great masters, the perfumes, warm and sweet, of swinging censers, and the delightful songs of silvery voices, all that may shock by its worldly aspect the ascetic and austere monk; but nothing is more beautiful, to my mind, than a religion which appeals to the heart by such means as that. Why should priests wish to serve a jealous God? Religion is not a bird of prey; it is a compassionate dove, which soars peacefully over all dreams and all loves.

LORENZO. Doubtless, what you say is perfectly true, and perfectly false, like all things in this world.

TEBALDEO FRECCIA *(approaching Valori)*. Ah, my Lord, how sweet it is to hear a man like your Eminence speak thus of tolerance and religious enthusiasm! Pardon a humble citizen, who is burning with divine fire, for thanking you for the words which he has just heard. To hear from the lips of a good man what one has in his own heart is the greatest happiness which one can desire.

VALORI. You are young Freccia, are you not?

TEBALDEO. My works have little merit; I know better how to love art than I know how to practice it. My entire youth has been spent in the churches. It seems to me that I can not admire Raphael and our divine Buonarotti anywhere else. So I spend whole days before their works, in unspeakable ecstasy. The strains of the organ reveal to me their thoughts and give me an insight into their minds. I look at the people in their paintings, so reverently kneeling, and I imagine that the songs of the choir emanate from their parted lips; that the clouds of aromatic incense pass between them and me in a light vapor. I believe that I see there the glory of the artist; it is therefore a sad and sweet perfume, which would be but empty did it not mount up to God.

VALORI. You have the true heart of an artist. Come to my palace, and bring your palette and brushes with you when you come. I would like to have you do some work for me.

TEBALDEO. Your Eminence pays me too much honor. I am but a humble curate of the holy religion of painting.

LORENZO. Why do you decline our offers of service? It seems to me that you have a frame in your hands.

TEBALDEO. It is true; but I dare not show it to such critical judges. It is a poor sketch of a magnificent dream.

LORENZO. You paint pictures of your dreams? I will have some of mine pose for you.

TEBALDEO. The life of an artist is devoted to the realization of his dreams. The greatest have represented theirs in all their force, with nothing changed. Their imagination was a fertile tree; the buds were easily transformed into flowers, and the flowers into fruit; presently the fruit ripened under a kindly sun, and when they were ripe they detached themselves and fell to earth without losing a particle of their virginal bloom. Alas! the dreams of mediocre artists are plants difficult to nourish, which one waters with very bitter tears to make them thrive at all. *(He snows his picture.)*

VALORI. Without flattery, that is beautiful: not of the first merit, it is true. Why should I flatter a man who does not flatter himself? But your wings have not sprouted yet, young man.

LORENZO. Is it a landscape, or a portrait? Should it be viewed lengthwise, or crosswise?

TEBALDEO. Your Lordship is laughing at me. It is a view of the Campo-Santo.

LORENZO. How far is it from here to immortality?

VALORI. It is wrong of you to tease that child. See how his great eyes grow more sad at each one of your jests.

TEBALDEO. Immortality is faith. Those to whom God has given wings arrive there joyously.

VALORI. You talk like a pupil of Raphael.

TEBALDEO. My Lord, he was my master. What I have learned I owe to him.

LORENZO. Come to my house. I want you to paint me a nude of La Mazzafirra.

TEBALDEO. I do not respect my brush, but I respect my art. I can not paint the portrait of a courtesan.

LORENZO. God took pains to make her; you might take enough to paint her picture. Would you like to paint a picture of Florence for me?

TEBALDEO. Yes, my Lord.

LORENZO. From what point would you do it?

TEBALDEO. From the east side of the city, on the left bank of the Arno. It is from that point that the perspective is broadest and most pleasing.

LORENZO. You would paint Florence, the squares, the buildings, and the streets?

TEBALDEO. Yes, my Lord.

LORENZO. Now why would you not paint a courtesan, if you would paint a bad place?

TEBALDEO. I have not yet been taught to speak thus of my mother.

LORENZO. Who do you call your mother?

TEBALDEO. Florence, my Lord.

LORENZO. Then you are a bastard, for your mother is nothing but a harlot.

TEBALDEO. A bleeding wound may breed corruption in the healthiest body; but the precious drops of my mother's blood flow from a sweet-smelling plant which heals all ills. Art, that divine flower, has sometimes need of a fertilizer to enrich the soil that bears it.

LORENZO. What do you mean by that?

TEBALDEO. Peaceful and happy nations have sometimes burned with a clear but feeble light. There are several strings to an angel's harp; a gentle zeyphr may play across the weakest ones, and draw from their accord a sweet and delicious harmony; but the silver string responds only to the passage of the north wind. It is the most beautiful and the noblest; and yet the touch of a rude hand is favorable to it. Enthusiasm goes hand in hand with suffering.

LORENZO. That is to say that an unhappy people begets great artists. I would like to be the alchemist of your alembic; the tears of the people would there be distilled into pearls. By the death of Satan! you please me. Families may mourn, nations die of misery, all that for the amusement of kings! An admirable poet! How do you reconcile all that with your religion?

TEBALDEO. I do not make sport of the unhappiness of families. I say that poesy is the mildest form of suffering, and that she loves her sisters. I pity unhappy people; but I believe, indeed, that they create great artists. Battlefields cause harvests to grow; corrupt worlds beget celestial fruit.

LORENZO. Your doublet is worn; would you like one like my livery?

TEBALDEO. I belong to no one. When thought wishes to be free, the body must be so too.

LORENZO. I have a mind to order my footman to give you a good beating.

TEBALDEO. Why, my Lord?

LORENZO. Because it strikes my fancy. Are you lame by birth, or by accident?

TEBALDEO. I am not lame. What do you mean by that?

LORENZO. You are either lame or else you are a fool.

TEBALDEO. Why, my Lord? You are making sport of me.

LORENZO. If you were not crippled, why would you remain, unless you are a fool, in a city where, by virtue of your ideas of liberty, the first valet of a Medicis could kill you without anybody finding any fault with it?

TEBALDEO. I love my mother Florence; that is why I stay here. I know that a citizen may be assassinated in the open street in broad daylight, according to the caprice of those who govern her; that is the reason that I carry this stiletto at my belt.

LORENZO. Would you stab the Duke, if the Duke were to stab you, as it has often happened that he has committed facetious murders for his own amusement?

TEBALDEO. I should kill him if he were to attack me.

LORENZO. You say that to me!

TEBALDEO. What would anybody want of me? I injure nobody. I spend my days at the studio. On Sunday I go to the Annonciade or to Sainte-Marie; the monks find that I have a voice; they dress me in a white robe and a red cap, and I take part in the choruses, sometimes a little solo: these are the only times that I appear in public. In the evening I go to see my mistress, and when the night is fine I pass it upon her balcony. Nobody knows me, and I know nobody. To whom would my life or my death be of use?

LORENZO. Are you a republican? Do you love princes?

TEBALDEO. I am an artist; I love my mother and my mistress.

LORENZO. Come to my palace to-morrow. I wish to order an important picture from you for my wedding-day.

(Exeunt.)

SCENE III

(House of the Marquise of Cibo.)

THE CARDINAL *(alone).* Yes, I will obey your orders, Farnese! That your apostolic commissioner may confine himself to the narrow circle of his office, I will shake with a firm hand the slippery ground upon which he does not dare to walk. You may depend upon me for that. I understand you, and I shall act secretly as you have commanded. You divined who I was when you placed me near to Alexander without investing me with any title which gave me any power over him. It is of another that he will rid himself, by obeying me unwittingly. That he may spend his force against the shadows of men swollen with the semblance of power, I will be the invisible link which will bind him hand and foot to the chain of which Rome and Caesar hold the two ends. If my eyes do not deceive me, there is in this house the hammer which will serve me. Alexander is in love with my sister-in-law; that she is flattered by that love is credible; what the result may be is doubtful; but what she means to do about it, that is what concerns me. Who knows how far the influence of an exalted woman might go, even with that coarse man, that living armor? Such a little sin for such a good cause; it is tempting, is it not, Ricciarda? To press that lion heart to your weak heart all pierced with bloody arrows, like that of Saint Sebastian; to plead with weeping eyes, while the adored tyrant passes his rude hands through your flowing locks; to strike the divine spark from a rock; surely that is worth the small sacrifice of matrimonial honor, and of a few other trifles. Florence would gain so much by it, while these good husbands lose nothing! But you should not take me for a confessor. Here she comes now, her prayer-book in her hand. So today all will be elucidated; simply whisper your secret into the ear of the priest: the courtier will be able to profit thereby; but, in all conscience, he will say nothing about it.

(Enter the Marquise of Cibo.)

THE CARDINAL *(seating himself).* I am ready.

(The Marquise kneels beside him upon her prie-dieu.)

THE MARQUISE. Bless me, my father, because I have sinned.

THE CARDINAL. Have you said your Confiteor? We can begin, Marquise.

THE MARQUISE. I accuse myself of fits of anger, of irreligious and injurious doubts against our Holy Father, the Pope.

THE CARDINAL. Go on.

THE MARQUISE. I said yesterday, in public, apropos of the Bishop of Fano, that the Holy Catholic Church was a place of debauchery.

THE CARDINAL. Go on.

THE MARQUISE. I have listened to conversations contrary to my marriage vows.

THE CARDINAL. Who held these conversations with you?

THE MARQUISE. I have read a letter written with the same thought.

THE CARDINAL. Who wrote you that letter?

THE MARQUISE. I am confessing what I have done, and not what others have done.

THE CARDINAL. My daughter, you must answer me, if you wish me to be able to give you perfect absolution. In the first place, tell me if you answered that letter.

THE MARQUISE. I answered it by word of mouth, but not in writing.

THE CARDINAL. What did you reply?

THE MARQUISE. I granted the person who wrote it permission to see me, as he requested.

THE CARDINAL. What took place at that interview?

THE MARQUISE. I blamed myself for having already listened to conversations prejudicial to my honor.

THE CARDINAL. How did you make that self-accusation?

THE MARQUISE. As a self-respecting woman should.

THE CARDINAL. Did you not allow it to be seen that a person might end in persuading you?

THE MARQUISE. No, Father.

THE CARDINAL. Did you announce to the person in question a determination to listen to no such conversations in future?

THE MARQUISE. Yes, Father.

THE CARDINAL. Does this person please you?

THE MARQUISE. My heart is not involved, I hope.

THE CARDINAL. Have you informed your husband?

THE MARQUISE. No, Father. A virtuous woman ought not to disturb her household with such stories as that.

THE CARDINAL. Are you hiding nothing from me? Did nothing pass between you and the person in question, which you hesitate to confide to me?

THE MARQUISE. Nothing, Father.

THE CARDINAL. Not a tender look, a stealthy kiss?

THE MARQUISE. No, Father.

THE CARDINAL. Are you sure, my daughter?

THE MARQUISE. Brother-in-law, it seems to me that I have not the habit of lying before God.

THE CARDINAL. You refused to tell me the name which I asked of you just now; I can not give you absolution, however, without knowing it.

THE MARQUISE. Why so? It may be a sin to read a letter, but not a signature. What matters the name?

THE CARDINAL. It matters more than you think.

THE MARQUISE. Malaspina, you want to know too much. Refuse me absolution, if you wish; I will take for a confessor the first priest who comes along, who will give it to me. *(She arises.)*

THE CARDINAL. What violence, Marquise! Do I not know that it is of the Duke that you are speaking?

THE MARQUISE. Of the Duke! Very well; if you know it, why do you wish to make me say it?

THE CARDINAL. Why do you refuse to say it to me? That astonishes me.

THE MARQUISE. And what do you want to do with it, my confessor? Is it to repeat it to my husband that you insist so strongly upon hearing it? Yes, this is very certain. It is wrong to have one of your relatives for a confessor. Heaven is my witness that in kneeling before you I forget that I am your sister-in-law; but you take pains to remind me of it. Be careful, Cibo, be careful for your eternal salvation, Cardinal though you are.

THE CARDINAL. Come back, Marquise; it is not as bad as you think.

THE MARQUISE. What do you mean?

THE CARDINAL. That a confessor ought to know everything, because he can manage everything, and that a brother-in-law ought to say nothing on certain conditions.

THE MARQUISE. What conditions?

THE CARDINAL. No, no, I am mistaken; that was not the word I meant to use. I meant that the Duke is powerful, that a rupture with him might injure the richest families; but that a secret of importance in experienced hands might become a source of abundant benefits.

THE MARQUISE. A source of benefits!... Experienced hands! I do not understand. What are you hiding, Cardinal, beneath those ambiguous words? There are certain phrases which sometimes pass the lips of you priests; a person does not know what to think of them.

THE CARDINAL. Come back and sit down, Ricciarda. I have not yet given you absolution.

THE MARQUISE. Talk away; I am not sure that I wish you to.

THE CARDINAL *(rising)*. You had better be careful, Marquise. When a person braves me to my face, he should have a solid and a flawless armor. I do not wish to threaten you; I have but one word to say to you: take another confessor. *(Exit.)*

THE MARQUISE *(alone)*. That is unheard-of! To go away with clenched fists and his eyes blazing with anger! To talk of experienced hands, of the direction to give to certain things! But what is the matter? That he might wish to penetrate my secret to inform my husband of it, I can readily understand; but if that is not his aim, what does he want to make of me? The Duke's mistress? To know everything and to manage everything did he say? That is impossible; there is some darker and more inexplicable mystery at the bottom of it. Cibo would never do a thing like that. No, I am sure of it; I know him too well. That would suit Lorenzaccio. But he... he must have had some secret meaning, greater and deeper than that. Ah, how men reveal themselves suddenly, after ten years of silence! It is frightful! Now, what shall I do? Do I love Alexander? No, surely I do not love him; I said so in my confession, and I told the truth. Why is Laurent at Massa? Why does the Duke urge me? Why did I say that I did not wish to see him again? Why? Ah, why is there in it all a magnet, an inexplicable charm which attracts me? *(She opens her window.)* How beautiful you are, Florence, but how sad! There is more than one house down there that Alexander has entered clandestinely by night. He is a libertine, I know. And why do you mingle with all this, Florence? Whom do I love? Is it you, or he?

AGNOLO *(entering).* Madame, his Highness has entered the courtyard.

THE MARQUISE. This is strange! Malaspina has quite unnerved me.

SCENE IV

(At the Soderini palace. Marie Soderini, Catherine, Lorenzo, seated.)

CATHERINE *(a book in her hand).* What story shall I read you, mother?

MARIE. My Cattina is making fun of her poor old mother. What do I know about your Latin books?

CATHERINE. This is not a Latin book, but it is a translation of one. It is the History of Rome.

LORENZO. I am very strong in Roman history. There was once a young nobleman named Tarquinius the Proud.

CATHERINE. Ah, that is a bloody story.

LORENZO. Not at all; it is a fairy story. Brutus was nothing but a fool, a monomaniac. Tarquinius was a duke full of wisdom, who went in slippered feet to see if young girls were asleep.

CATHERINE. Do you also speak idly of Lucretia?

LORENZO. She gave herself the pleasure of sin, and the glory of death. She allowed herself to be taken alive like lark in a snare, and then she very gracefully plunged a dagger into her breast.

MARIE. If you despise women, why do you seek to lower them in the eyes of your mother and sister?

LORENZO. I esteem you and her. Aside from that, society inspires me with horror.

MARIE. Do you know the dream I had last night, my child?

LORENZO. What dream?

MARIE. It was not a dream, for I was not asleep. I was alone in this great room; the lamp was far from me, upon that table by the window. I was thinking of the days when I used to be happy, of the days of your childhood, my Lorenzino. I observed the dark night, and I said to myself: He will not return until morning, he who used to spend his nights in study. My eyes filled with tears, and I shook my head as I felt them flowing. Suddenly I heard footsteps in the corridor. I turned around; a man clad in black, with a book under his arm, was coming toward me: it was you, Renzo. "You are back early!" I exclaimed. But the specter seated itself beside the lamp without replying; it opened its book, and I recognized my Lorenzo of olden times.

LORENZO. You saw it?

MARIE. As plainly as I see you.

LORENZO. When did it go away?

MARIE. When you rang the bell this morning as you came in.

LORENZO. My specter! And it went away when I returned?

MARIE. It arose with a melancholy air, and vanished like a morning vapor.

LORENZO. Catherine, Catherine, read me the story of Brutus.

CATHERINE. What is the matter with you? You are trembling from head to foot.

LORENZO. Mother, take a seat this evening in the same place where you were last night, and if my specter returns, say to it that it will see something by and by that will astonish it.

(Somebody knocks.)

CATHERINE. It is Uncle Bindo and Baptista Venturi.

(Bindo and Venturi enter.)

MARIE. We will leave you; God grant that you may succeed!

(Exit with Catherine.)

BINDO. Lorenzo, why do you not deny that scandalous story that people are telling about you?

LORENZO. What story?

BINDO. They say that you fainted at the sight of a sword.

LORENZO. Do you believe them, uncle?

BINDO. I saw you fence at Rome; but it would not surprise me if you were to become viler than a dog, with the life you are leading here.

LORENZO. The story is true. I did faint away. Good morning, Venturi. What is the price of goods? How is business?

VENTURI. My Lord, I am at the head of a silk factory; but it is an insult to call me a tradesman.

LORENZO. True, I only meant that you had contracted at college the innocent habit of selling silk.

BINDO. I have confided to Signor Venturi the plans which are occupying so many families in Florence at this time. He is a worthy friend of liberty, and I mean, Lorenzo, that you shall treat him as such. The time to joke is past. You have sometimes said to us that that extreme confidence which the Duke shows toward you was only a snare on your part. Is that true, or false? Are you on our side, or are you not? That is what we must know. All the great families see plainly that the despotism of the Medicis is neither just nor tolerable. "By what right should we allow that proud house to arise peacefully over the ruins of our privileges? The capitulation is violated. The power of Germany makes itself felt more absolutely from day to day. It is time to put an end to it and to reassemble the patriots. Will you respond to that appeal?

LORENZO. What have you to say about it, Venturi? Speak, speak; see, my uncle is recovering his breath; seize this opportunity, if you love your country.

VENTURI. My Lord, I think the same, and I have not a word to add.

LORENZO. Not a word? Not one pretty, little, sonorous word? You are familiar with true eloquence. You can turn a great sentence around one pretty little word, neither too short nor too long, and as round as a top; you throw back your left arm in a manner to impart dignity and grace to the folds of your mantle; you let loose your sentence, which unwinds like a vibrant string, and the little top is off with a delicious hum. You could almost pick it up in the palm of your hand, as children in the street do.

BINDO. You are an insolent fellow! Either reply to our questions, or leave the room.

LORENZO. I am one with you, uncle. Do you not see, by the manner in which I wear my hair, that I am a republican at heart? Look how my beard is trimmed. Doubt not for a moment that patriotism breathes through the innermost recesses of my being.

(The door-bell rings; the courtyard fills with horses and pages.)

A Page *(entering)*. The Duke.

(Enter Alexander.)

Lorenzo. What an excess of favor, Prince! You deign to visit a humble servant in person?

The Duke. Who are these men? I want to speak with you.

Lorenzo. I have the honor of presenting to your Lordship my uncle, Signer Bindo Altoviti, who regrets that a long sojourn at Naples has prevented him from paying his respects to you before. This other gentleman is the distinguished Signor Baptista Venturi, who manufactures silk, it is true, but does not sell it. Do not let the unexpected presence of so great a Prince in this humble house disturb you, my dear uncle, nor you either, my worthy Venturi. Whatever you ask for will be granted, Or you will have the right to say that my supplications have no influence with my gracious Sovereign.

The Duke. What do you want, Bindo?

Bindo. My Lord, I am very sorry that my nephew...

Lorenzo. The title of Ambassador to Rome belongs to nobody just now. My uncle hopes to obtain it through your kindness. There is not in all Florence a man who could bear comparison with him, when it is a question of the devotion and respect due to the Medicis.

The Duke. Indeed, Renzino? Very well! my dear Bindo, that is settled. Come to the palace to-morrow morning.

Bindo. My Lord, I am overwhelmed! How to repay you...

Lorenzo. Signer Venturi, although he doesn't sell silk, asks a privilege for his factories.

The Duke. What privilege?

Lorenzo. Your arms upon the door, with the license. Grant it to him, my Lord, if you love those that love you.

The Duke. All right. Is that all? Go, gentlemen; and peace go with you.

Venturi. My Lord... you overwhelm me with joy...I can't express.

The Duke *(to his guards)*. Allow these two people to pass.

Bindo *(aside to Venturi as they go off)*. That was a scurvy trick.

Venturi *(aside)*. What are you going to do about it?

Bindo *(aside)*. What the deuce would you have me do? I am appointed.

Venturi *(aside)*. It is terrible!

(Exeunt.)

The Duke. The Marquise has yielded.

LORENZO. I am sorry.

THE DUKE. Why?

LORENZO. Because that will be prejudicial to others.

THE DUKE. In faith, no; I am tired of her already. Tell me, my dear boy, who is that pretty woman who is tending her flowers at that window? For a long time I have seen her every time I pass.

LORENZO. Where?

THE DUKE. In the palace across the street.

LORENZO. Oh! that's nothing.

THE DUKE. Nothing? Do you call those arms nothing? My word, what a Venus!

LORENZO. She is a neighbor of mine.

THE DUKE. I wish to speak to that neighbor. Ah, zounds! it is Catharine Ginori, if I am not mistaken.

LORENZO. No.

THE DUKE. I recognize her very well; she is your aunt. Pest! I had forgotten that fact. Bring her to supper.

LORENZO. That is easier said than done. She is a virtuous girl.

THE DUKE. Go on! Is there such a thing with us?

LORENZO. I will ask her, if you wish; but I warn you that she is a blue-stocking; she speaks Latin.

THE DUKE. All right! She does not make love in Latin. Come this way; we can see her better from this gallery.

LORENZO. Some other time, your Highness. I must go to Strozzi's, and I have no time to lose.

THE DUKE. What! to that old fool?

LORENZO. Yes, to that old wretch's. It seems that he can not cure himself of that strange whim for opening his purse to all these vile creatures called exiles, and that the beggars assemble at his door every day, before putting on their shoes and taking up their cudgels. My plan now is to hasten to dine with this old jail-bird, and renew the assurance of my cordial friendship. I shall have some good story to tell you this evening, some delightful little prank which will make some of those rascals rise early to-morrow morning.

THE DUKE. How fortunate it is that I have you, my dear boy! I confess that I do not understand why they receive you.

LORENZO. Nonsense! If you only knew how easy it is to draw the wool over the eyes of a blockhead! It must be that you have never tried. By the way, did you not tell me that you wished to give your portrait I forget to whom? I have a painter to bring to you, a protégé of mine.

THE DUKE. Very well; but do not forget your aunt. It was on her account that I came to see you. The devil take me! I can not forget your aunt.

LORENZO. And the Marquise?

THE DUKE. Talk to me of your aunt, I tell you.

(Exeunt.)

SCENE V

(A room at the Strozzi Palace. Philippe Strozzi. The Prior, Louise occupied with some needlework; Lorenzo, lying upon a sofa.)

PHILIPPE. God grant that nothing come of it. How many inextinguishable, implacable hatreds have not begun otherwise! An insulting speech, the fumes of a revel upon the maudlin lips of some debauchee! That is the way family feuds begin, that is the way daggers are drawn. Somebody is insulted, and he kills; somebody kills, and he gets killed in turn. By and by the hatred takes deep root; sons are cradled in the coffins of their ancestors, and whole generations spring up with sword in hand.

THE PRIOR. Perhaps it was wrong of me to remember that vile speech and this accursed journey to Mount Olivet; but how can a body stand these Salviatis?

PHILIPPE. Ah, Leon, Leon! I ask you, what difference would it have made with Louise and ourselves even if you had said nothing to my children? Can not the virtue of a Strozzi forget the idle word of a Salviati? Should the inhabitants of a marble palace know the obscenities that the populace write upon their walls? What matters the speech of a Julien? Will my daughter be less able to find a worthy husband because of it? Will her children respect her less? Shall I remember it as I kiss her good night? What are we coming to, if the insolence of a nobody unsheathes swords like ours? Now the fat is in the fire; there is Pierre furious at what you told us. He has taken the field; he has gone to the Pazzis. God knows what will happen! If he should meet Salviati, blood will be spilled; my blood upon the stones of Florence! Ah, why am I a father!

THE PRIOR. If somebody had reported to me an insult about my sister, whatever it was, I should have given him the cold shoulder, and all would have ended there; but this one was addressed to me; it

41

was so gross that I imagined the boor did not know of whom he was speaking; but he knew very well.

PHILIPPE. Yes, they know, base wretches! They know very well where they strike! The trunk of an old tree is of too hard a fiber; they will not touch that. But they know the delicate fiber which trembles in its heart when they attack its weakest branch. My Louise! Ah, what was the motive? My hands tremble at that idea! Just God, is the reason for that, old age?

THE PRIOR. Pierre is too hot-headed.

PHILIPPE. Poor Pierre! how the blood mounted to his brow! How he shook, in listening to the account of the insult paid to his sister! I was a fool for allowing you to tell it. Pierre walked the floor with great strides, restless, furious, beside himself; he walked to and fro as I am doing now. I looked at him in silence: it is such a fine sight to see the pure blood mounting to a blameless brow! I thought, "O, my country! there is one, and he is my first-born." Ah, Leon, it is of no use, I am a Strozzi.

THE PRIOR. Perhaps there is not as much danger as you think. It is a great chance if he meets Salviati this evening. To-morrow he will see everything more soberly.

PHILIPPE. Have no doubt of it; Pierre will either kill him or perish in the attempt. *(He opens the window.)* Where are they now? It is night; the city is wrapped in darkness; those somber streets inspire me with horror; blood is flowing somewhere; I am sure of it.

THE PRIOR. Calm yourself.

PHILIPPE. By the manner in which Pierre went away I am sure that he will only return revenged or dead. I saw him take down his sword with a look of determination on his face. He was biting his lips, and the muscles of his arms were like whip-cords. Yes, yes, by this time he is either dead or avenged; there is no doubt about it.

THE PRIOR. Reassure yourself; close that window.

PHILIPPE. Well, Florence, teach thus to thy pavements the color of my noble blood. It flows in the veins of forty of your sons. And I, the head of this great family, more than once again my gray head will lean from these high windows in paternal anguish. More than once that blood, which you perhaps are indifferently drinking at this very hour, will dry in the sunshine of your public squares! But do not laugh to-night at poor old Strozzi, who has fears for his child. Be sparing of his family, for there will come a day when you will depend upon it, when you will place yourself with him at the window, and your heart will also beat when you shall hear the sound of our swords.

LOUISE. Father! father! you frighten me!

THE PRIOR *(aside to Louise).* Is that not Thomas who is prowling around those lampposts? It seems to me that I recognize him by his short stature. Now he has gone away.

PHILIPPE. Poor city! where fathers await thus the return of their children! Poor country! poor country! There are many more at this hour who have donned their mantles and swords to plunge out into the dark night; and those who await them are not anxious; they know that they will die to-morrow of want, if they do not die of cold to-night. And we, in these sumptuous palaces, wait until we are insulted before drawing our swords! The vile speech of some drunken wretch transports us with rage, and disperses our sons and our friends into the somber streets! The dust upon our firearms is not disturbed for public misfortunes. They think Philippe Strozzi an honest man because he does right without putting a stop to the wrong; and now, I, a father, what would I not give if there were a being in the world capable of restoring to me my son, and of meting out just punishment for this insult to my daughter! But why should people prevent misfortune from coming to me, when I have not prevented it from coming to others, and that, too, when I had it in my power? I have pored over my books, and dreamed for my country that which I most admired in antiquity. The very walls around me cried out for vengeance, and I stopped up my ears to bury myself in my meditations! It has been necessary for tyranny to slap me in the face in order to make me say, "Let us act!" And my vengeance comes late.

(Enter Pierre, Thomas, and Francois Pazzi.)

PIERRE. The deed is done; Salviati is dead. *(He kisses his sister.)*

LOUISE. How horrible! You are covered with blood!

PIERRE. We waited for him at the corner of Archer Street. François stopped his horse, Thomas stabbed him in the leg, and I...

LOUISE. Hush! hush! You terrify me! Your eyes are starting out of their sockets; your hands are hideous, and you are as pale as death.

LORENZO *(rising).* You are glorious, Pierre! you are as great as vengeance.

PIERRE. Who said that? You here, in this house, Lorenzaccio? *(He goes up to his father.)* When are you going to close your doors to that scoundrel? Do you not know well enough what he is, to say nothing of the story of his duel with Maurice?

PHILIPPE. That is all right; I know all about it. If Lorenzo is here, it is because I have good reasons for receiving him. We will talk about that at a suitable time and place.

PIERRE. Humph! reasons for receiving that scoundrel? I shall easily find a very good one for pitching him out of the window one of these fine days. Say what you like, it suffocates me to see such a leper in this room, lounging upon our furniture.

PHILIPPE. Nonsense—peace! You are a madcap! God grant that your act of this evening be followed by no evil consequences to us! You must hide yourself, to begin with.

PIERRE. Hide myself! In the name of all the saints, why should I hide myself?

LORENZO *(to Thomas)*. So you hit him on the shoulder?... Tell me a little...

(He leads him into the recess of a window; the two converse in a low voice.)

PIERRE. No, father, I will not hide myself. The insult was public; he gave it to us in a public place. I struck him down in the middle of the street, and it is advisable to tell everybody of it to-morrow morning. Since when does a man hide himself for vindicating his honor? I would willingly wander about with drawn sword, all covered with blood, and so proclaim it to the whole world.

PHILIPPE. Come away; I must talk to you. You are not wounded, my child? You escaped without any injury?

(Exeunt.)

SCENE VI

(At the palace of the Duke. The Duke, half clad, Tebaldeo, painting his portrait; Giomo is playing the guitar.)

GIOMO *(singing).*

> Carry my heart to my love,
> Cup-bearer, when I am dead;
> Of masses, orations, and prayers,
> Let not a one be said.

THE DUKE. I knew there was something I wanted to ask you. Tell me, Hungarian, what did you do to the fellow I saw you beating so lustily?

GIOMO. Faith, I can not say, nor he either.

THE DUKE. Why, is he dead?

GIOMO. He was a blackguard from a house in the neighborhood; just now, in passing, it appeared to me as though they were burying him.

THE DUKE. When my Giomo strikes, he strikes hard.

GIOMO. It pleases you to say that. I have seen you kill a man at a blow more than once.

THE DUKE. You believe it? Was I drunk? When I am in high spirits, my lightest blows are deadly. What is the matter with you, young man does your hand shake? You are leering terribly!

TEBALDEO. Nothing, my Lord, please your Highness.

(Enter Lorenzo.)

LORENZO. How is it getting along? Are you pleased with my protégé? *(He takes the Duke's coat of mail from the sofa.)* This is a fine coat of mail, your Highness! But it must be very warm.

THE DUKE. Indeed, if it were uncomfortable I should not wear it. But it is made of steel wire; the sharpest blade could not puncture a mesh of it, and at the same time it is as light as silk. There is not another like it, perhaps, in all Europe; therefore I shall scarcely leave it off; never, to speak more plainly.

LORENZO. It is very light, but very strong. Do you believe it would be proof against a stiletto?

THE DUKE. Certainly.

LORENZO. Oh, yes, I remember now; you always wear it under your doublet. The other day, at the chase, as I was riding in croup behind you, I felt it distinctly as I was holding you around the waist with my arms. It is a prudent habit.

THE DUKE. It is not that I mistrust any one; as you say, it is a habit—simply the habit of a Soldier.

LORENZO. Your costume is magnificent! How nice these gloves smell! Why do you pose half naked? This coat of mail would have made a fine effect in your portrait. You were wrong to leave it off.

THE DUKE. It was the painter's wish; moreover, it is always better to pose with bare neck: look at the antiques.

LORENZO. Where the deuce is my guitar? I must play a second to Giomo. *(Exit.)*

TEBALDEO. I will paint no more to-day, my Lord.

GIOMO *(at the window).* What is Lorenzo doing? There he is, looking down in the well in the middle of the garden: it seems to me that it is not there that he should be looking for his guitar.

THE DUKE. Give me my clothes. Where is my coat of mail?

GIOMO. I don't find it; I have looked everywhere. It must have taken wings.

THE DUKE. Lorenzo had it not five minutes ago; he must have thrown it into a corner when he went away, conformably to his usual praiseworthy habit of laziness.

GIOMO. This is incredible; no more coat of mail than in my hand.

THE DUKE. Nonsense! you must be dreaming; that is impossible.

GIOMO. See for yourself, my Lord; the room is not so large!

THE DUKE. Renzo had it there, upon that sofa.

(Reenter Lorenzo.)

THE DUKE. What have you done with my coat of mail? We can not find it anywhere.

LORENZO. I put it back where it was. Wait! No, I placed it on that chair; no, it was on the bed. I know nothing about it; but I have found my guitar. *(He sings to his own accompaniment)*

Good morning, Madam Abbess…

GIOMO. At the bottom of the well, apparently, for you were bending over it just now, with an air of great absorption.

LORENZO. To spit into a well to make circles is my greatest pleasure. Aside from drinking and sleeping, I have no other occupation. *(He continues to play.)*

Good morning, good morning,
Mistress of my heart.

THE DUKE. It is unheard-of that that coat should be lost! I believe I never took it off twice in my life, excepting when I went to bed.

LORENZO. Nonsense! nonsense! Do not make a valet of a pope's son. Your servants will find it.

THE DUKE. The devil take you! It was you that mislaid it.

LORENZO. If I were Duke of Florence, I should concern myself with other things than coats of mail. By the way, I spoke of you to my dear aunt. Everything is all right. Come and sit here a little while; I want to whisper to you.

GIOMO *(low to the Duke).* It is singular, to say the least; the coat of mail has been carried off.

THE DUKE. Somebody will find it. *(He seats himself beside Lorenzo.)*

GIOMO *(aside)*. It is not natural to leave good company to go and spit into a well. I would like to find that coat of mail, to remove from my head an old idea which gets rusty from time to time. Bah! a Lorenzaccio! The coat is on some chair.

SCENE VII

(In front of the palace. Enter Salviati covered with blood and limping; two men support him.)

SALVIATI *(shouting.)* Alexander de Medicis! open your window, and see how people treat your servants!

THE DUKE *(at the window)*. Who is there in the mud? Who crawls to my palace walls with such frightful cries?

SALVIATI. The Strozzis have assassinated me; I am dying at your door.

THE DUKE. Which of the Strozzis, and why?

SALVIATI. Because I said that their sister was in love with you, my noble Duke. The Strozzis thought their sister insulted because I said that you pleased her; three of them assassinated me. I recognized Pierre and Thomas; I did not know the third one.

THE DUKE. Have them bring you up here. By Hercules! the murderers shall pass the night in jail, and we will hang them to-morrow morning.

(Salviati enters the palace.)

ACT THE THIRD

SCENE I

(Lorenzo's bedroom. Lorenzo, Scoronconcolo, fencing.)

SCORONCONCOLO. Have you played enough, sir?

LORENZO. No; cry louder. There, parry that! there, die! Take that, wretch!

SCORONCONCOLO. Ah, the assassin! He is killing me! He is cutting my throat!

LORENZO. Die! die! die! Stamp your foot.

SCORONCONCOLO. Help, archers! help! He is killing me, this demon of a Lorenzo!

LORENZO. Die, base wretch! I will stick you, pig... I will stick you! To the heart... to the heart! He is ripped open! Shout then... strike! kill! Open his heart! Cut him in pieces, and eat him... eat him! I am in to the elbow! Cut his throat, roll him... roll! Bite him... bite, and eat! *(He sinks exhausted.)*

SCORONCONCOLO. You have invented a rough play, master, and you go at it like a tiger... a thousand million thunderbolts! You roar like a cave full of lions and panthers.

LORENZO. Oh, day of blood! Oh, nuptial day! Oh, sun, sun! you have been dry long enough; you are dying of thirst, sun! His blood will intoxicate you. Oh, my vengeance! How long your nails are in sprouting! Oh, teeth of Ugolino; you need the skull... the skull!

SCORONCONCOLO. Are you delirious? Have you a fever, or are you yourself a dream?

LORENZO. Coward! coward! ruffian! The poor little one, the fathers, the daughters, farewells, endless farewells... the banks of the Arno full of farewells! The urchins write them upon the walls. Laugh, old man! laugh in your sleeve! Do you not see that my claws are sprouting? Ah, the skull... the skull! *(He swoons.)*

SCORONCONCOLO. Master, you have an enemy. *(He dashes water into his face.)* Come! master, it is not worth while to madden yourself so. A man has lofty sentiments or has them not. I shall never forget that you did me a good turn, without which I should be far from here. Master, if you have an enemy, say so; I will rid you of him without anybody being the wiser.

LORENZO. It is nothing. I tell you my only pleasure is to frighten my neighbors.

SCORONCONCOLO. Ever since we have been making such an uproar in this room, and turning everything in it topsy-turvy, they ought to be very well accustomed to our racket. I believe that you could cut the throats of thirty men in the corridor, and roll them over your floor, without anybody in the house noticing that anything unusual was happening. If you wish to frighten your neighbors, you go about it badly. They were frightened the first time, it is true; but now they content themselves with getting angry, and do not even take the pains to leave their seats or open their windows.

LORENZO. Do you believe it?

SCORONCONCOLO. You have an enemy, master. Have I not seen you stamp the earth, and curse the day you were born? Have I not ears? And in the midst of your ragings, have I not distinctly heard the clear tinkling of one little word, revenge? Upon my word, sir, you are growing thin; you do not joke as you used to. Believe me, there is nothing so bad for the digestion as a bitter hatred. Between two men in sunlight, is there not always one whose shadow annoys the other? Your physician is in my scabbard; let me cure you. *(He draws his sword.)*

LORENZO. Has that physician ever cured you?

SCORONCONCOLO. Four or five times. There was once a young lady at Padua who said to me...

LORENZO. Show me that sword. Ah, blackguard, it is a fine blade!

SCORONCONCOLO. Try it, and you will see.

LORENZO. You have guessed my malady; I have an enemy. But for him I will not use a sword that has been used for others. That which shall kill him must have but one baptism here below; it will guard his name.

SCORONCONCOLO. What is the name of that man?

LORENZO. What does it matter? Are you devoted to me?

SCORONCONCOLO. For you I would recrucify the Christ!

LORENZO. I tell you this in confidence, I shall do the deed in this chamber. Listen attentively and make no mistake. If I lay him low at the first stroke, do not dare to lay a hand upon him. But I am no bigger than a flea, and he is a wild boar. If he defends himself, I count upon you to hold his hands; nothing more do you understand? It is my affair. I will give you warning of the time and place.

SCORONCONCOLO. Amen!

SCENE II

(At the Strozzi Palace.)

PIERRE. When I think of it, I have a desire to cut off my right hand. To have missed that scoundrel! A blow so accurate, and to have missed him! To whom would it not have been a service to be able to say to people, "There is one less Salviati in the world?" The knave did as spiders do he drew in his hooked legs as he fell, and feigned death for fear of being finished.

PHILIPPE. What matters it to you that he lives? Your revenge is only the more complete because of it.

PIERRE. Yes, I know very well that is how you look at things. There, father, you are a good patriot, but a still better father of a family: do not trouble your head about all this.

PHILIPPE. What have you in your head now? Can you not live a quarter of an hour without thinking of mischief?

PIERRE. No, by the infernal! I can not keep quiet a quarter of an hour in this poisonous atmosphere. It weighs upon my head like the vault of a prison, and it seems to me that I breathe the foul breath of drunkards. Good-by, I have some business to attend to now.

PHILIPPE. Where are you going?

PIERRE. Why do you want to know? I am going to the Pazzis.

PHILIPPE. Wait for me, then, for I am going there too.

PIERRE. Not now, father; it is not a good time for you.

PHILIPPE. Speak frankly to me, Pierre.

PIERRE. This is between ourselves, There are some fifty of us, the Ruccellais and others, who have no love for the bastard.

PHILIPPE. So then?

PIERRE. So then avalanches sometimes occur by means of a pebble no larger than the end of a finger.

PHILIPPE. But have you formed any resolutions, any plans? Have you taken any steps? Oh, children, children! to play with life and death! Questions which have shaken the earth to its foundations, ideas which have whitened myriads of heads, and which have caused them to roll like grains of sand at the feet of the executioner; projects which Providence itself regards with fear and trembling, and leaves to man's accomplishing without daring to interfere! You discuss these things while fencing, or in drinking a glass of wine, as though it were a question of a horse or a masquerade! Do you know the meaning of the word republic, of the artisan at his work-bench, of the laborer in the field, of the citizen at his post, of the whole life of a realm? The welfare of men, God of justice! Oh, children, children! have you counted the cost?

PIERRE. A good thrust of a lancet heals all ills.

PHILIPPE. To heal! to heal! Do you know that the least thrust of a lancet should be given by a skilful hand? Do you know that it requires life-long experience, and world-wide knowledge, to draw from the arm of a sick man a single drop of blood? Was I not shocked, therefore, when I saw you thrust your naked sword beneath your cloak last night? Am I not the father of my Louise, as you are her brother? Was it not a just vengeance? And yet, do you know what it cost me? Ah, fathers know that, but the children! If you are ever a father we will talk about it.

PIERRE. You who know how to love, ought to know how to hate.

PHILIPPE. What have those Pazzis done to God? They invite their friends to come and conspire, as one invites to a game of dice, and the friends as they enter their courtyard, slip in the blood of their grandfathers. For what are their swords thirsting? What do you want? What do you want?

PIERRE. Why do you belie yourself? Haven't I heard you say a hundred times what we are saying now? Do we not know what you are doing, when your servants see your evening lamps still burning at your windows when they arise in the morning? They who pass sleepless nights do not sleep silently.

PHILIPPE. What are you driving at? Tell me.

PIERRE. The Medicis are a pestilence. He who is bitten by a serpent has only to set up for a doctor; he has only to cauterize the wound.

PHILIPPE. And when you have overthrown existing conditions, what will you put in their place?

PIERRE. We are always sure of finding nothing worse.

PHILIPPE. I tell you count well the cost.

PIERRE. The heads of a hydra are easily counted.

PHILIPPE. And you intend to act? That is decided?

PIERRE. We intend to hamstring the murderers of Florence.

PHILIPPE. That is irrevocable?... You intend to act?

PIERRE. Good-by, father; let me go alone.

PHILIPPE. Since when does the old eagle stay in the nest, when his eaglets go to the quarry? Oh, my children, my brave and beautiful youth! You who have the strength that I have lost, you who are to-day what young Philippe used to be, allow him to grow old for you! Take me along, my son; I see that you are going to act. I will not preach you a long sermon; I will only say a few words. There ought to be a little wisdom in this gray head: two words, and I am done. I am not raving any more; I will not be a burden to you. Do not go without me, my child; wait till I get my cloak.

PIERRE. Come, my noble father; we will kiss the hem of your garment. You are our patriarch; come and see the dreams of your life realized. Liberty is ripe; come and see the plant which you love arise from the earth.

(Exeunt.)

SCENE III

(A street. A German Officer and Soldiers; Thomas Strozzi in their midst.)

THE OFFICER. If you do not find him at home, we will find him at the Strozzis.

THOMAS. Go your way, and do not trouble yourself; you will know what it costs.

THE OFFICER. No threats. I am executing the orders of the Duke, and I will take nothing from anybody.

THOMAS. Imbecile! Who arrests a Strozzi upon the word of a Medicis!

(A group gathers around them.)

A CITIZEN. Why do you arrest this gentleman? We are very well acquainted with him; he is Philippe's son.

ANOTHER CITIZEN. Let him go; we will be responsible for him.

FIRST CITIZEN. Yes, yes, we will answer for the Strozzis. Let him go, or look out for your ears.

THE OFFICER. Be off, rascals! Let the Duke's justice pass, if you do not like the blows of a halberd.

(Pierre and Philippe arrive.)

PIERRE. What is the matter? What is the row? What are you doing there, Thomas?

THE CITIZENS. Prevent him, Philippe; he wants to take your son to jail.

PHILIPPE. To jail? Upon whose order?

PIERRE. To jail? Do you know whom you are dealing with?

THE OFFICER. Arrest that man! *(The soldiers arrest Pierre.)*

PIERRE. Let go of me, wretches, or I will stick you like pigs.

PHILIPPE. By what authority do you act, sir?

THE OFFICER *(showing the Duke's order).* There is my warrant. I have an order to arrest Pierre and Thomas Strozzi.

(The soldiers press back the people., who throw stones at them.)

PIERRE. Of what are we accused? What have we done? Help me, my friends; let us thrash this rabble. *(He draws his sword.)*

(Another detachment of soldiers arrives.)

THE OFFICER. Come here; come to my assistance.

(Pierre is disarmed.)

THE OFFICER. March! and the first who comes too close, let him have the thrust of a pike in his belly! That will teach them to mind their own business.

PIERRE. Nobody has a right to arrest me without an order from the Council of Eight. I care nothing about the orders of Alexander. Where is the order of the Eight?

THE OFFICER. It is before them that we are taking you.

PIERRE. If it is before them, I have nothing to say. Of what am I accused?

A VOICE IN THE CROWD. What, Philippe, you allow your children to be taken to the tribunal of the Eight!

PIERRE. Answer me, of what am I accused?

THE OFFICER. That does not concern me.

(The soldiers go off with Pierre and Thomas.)

PIERRE *(leaving).* Do not be at all uneasy, father; the Eight will send me back to supper at the house, and the bastard will have to pay the costs of the court.

PHILIPPE *(alone, seating himself upon a bench).* I have many children, but not for long, if this continues. What are we coming to, if a vengeance as just as Heaven is punished as a crime! What! the two oldest of a family as old as the hills, imprisoned like highway robbers! The grossest insult chastised, a Salviati struck, and the halberds in play! Come out of the scabbard, my sword! If the sacred apparel of judicial execution becomes the breastplate of ruffians and drunkards, may the ax and poniard, the arms of the assassin, protect the honest man. O, Christ! Does justice become a go-between! The honor of the Strozzis affronted in a public place, and a tribunal obeying the quibbles of a boor! A Salviati throwing down his gauntlet all stained with wine and blood, to the noblest family of Florence, and when he is chastised, drawing the executioner's ax to his defense! Merciful heavens! I talked, not a quarter of an hour ago, against the ideas of rebellion, and this is the bread that I am given to eat, with the words of peace upon my lips! Come! rouse yourselves, my arms; and you, old body, bent with age and study, straighten yourself for action!

(Enter Lorenzo.)

LORENZO. Are you asking for alms, Philippe, sitting at this street corner?

PHILIPPE. I demand the charity of man's justice: I am a beggar thirsting for justice, and my honor is in tatters.

LORENZO. What change is being wrought in the world, and what new guise is nature to assume, if the mask of anger rests upon the august and peaceful face of old Philippe? Oh, my father! what are these lamentations? For whom do you scatter upon earth the most precious jewels under the sun, the tears of a man without fear and without reproach?

PHILIPPE. We must rid ourselves of the Medicis, Lorenzo. You are a Medicis yourself, but only in name; if I have understood you, if I have been an impassive and faithful spectator of the hideous comedy which you are playing, let the man emerge from the actor. If you have ever been anything that is honest, be so to-day. Pierre and Thomas are in prison.

LORENZO. Yes, yes, I know that.

PHILIPPE. Is that your reply? Is that your attitude, swordless man?

LORENZO. Tell me what you wish, then you shall have my reply.

PHILIPPE. To act! How, I do not know. What means to employ, what lever to place beneath that citadel of death, to raise and push it into the river; what to do, what to determine, what men to look for, I don't know yet. But to act, to act, to act! O, Lorenzo! The time has come. Are you not defamed, treated like a dog and a heartless wretch? If, in spite of all that, I have kept my door open to you, my heart and hand open to you, speak, and let me see whether I have been mistaken. Have you not talked to me of a man also called Lorenzo, who is hiding behind the Lorenzo that we see? Does not that man love his country? Is he not devoted to his friends? You said so, and I believed it. Speak, speak, the time has come.

LORENZO. If I am not such a one as you wish, may the sun fall upon my head!

PHILIPPE. Friend, it is wrong to laugh at a desperate old man. If you speak the truth, then, to arms! I have received promises from you which should be binding upon God himself, and it was in consequence of those promises that I received you. The role which you are playing is a role of mire and leprosy, such as the prodigal son would not have played in a day of madness, and yet I received you. When the very stones cried out at your passing, when every step of yours caused pools of human blood to spurt out, I called you by the sacred name of friend; I closed my ears to believe you, my eyes to love you; I allowed the shadow of your bad reputation to pass over my honor, and my children have distrusted me, in finding upon my palm the hideous outline of the contact of your hand. Be sincere, for I have been; act, for you are young, and I am old.

LORENZO. Pierre and Thomas are in prison; is that all?

PHILIPPE. O, heavens and earth! yes, that is all. Scarcely anything two children of my loins who are sitting upon the bench of thieves. Two heads that I have kissed as many times as I have gray hairs, and that I shall find nailed to the gate of the fortress to-morrow morning. Yes, that is all nothing more, in sooth.

LORENZO. Do not talk to me like that: I am consumed with a sadness compared to which the darkest night is a dazzling luminary.

(He seats himself beside Philippe.)

PHILIPPE. Do you not see that it is impossible for me to leave my children to die? They may tear me limb from limb, but, like the serpent, the mutilated fragments of Philippe would reunite and raise themselves up for vengeance. I know them so well, the Eight! A tribunal of statues! A forest of specters, over which there passes from time to time the dismal breath of doubt which stirs them for a moment, which resolves itself into a word without further appeal. A word, a word, a conscience! Those men eat, they sleep, they have wives and daughters! Ah! let them kill and let them slaughter, but not my children, not my children!

LORENZO. Pierre is a man; he will speak, and he will be set at liberty.

PHILIPPE. Oh, my Pierre, my first-born!

LORENZO. Go home and keep quiet; or, better yet, leave Florence. I will be responsible for everything, if you will leave Florence.

PHILIPPE. I an exile! I, in the bed of a public-house at my last hour! O, God! all that for a speech of a Salviati!

LORENZO. Be aware of this, Salviati wanted to seduce your daughter, but not for himself alone. Alexander has a foot in that man's bed; he exercises there the right of lordship over prostitution.

PHILIPPE. And we are doing nothing! O, Lorenzo, Lorenzo! You are a strong man; talk to me. I am weak, and my heart is too much interested in it all. I exhaust myself, you see. I have been too much given to reflection; I have been too self-centered, like a horse of the winepress; I am no longer fit for the fray. Tell me what you think; I will do it.

LORENZO. Go home, my dear sir.

PHILIPPE. This one thing is certain: I am going to the Pazzis; there are there fifty young men of determination. They have sworn to act. I will talk to them nobly, as a Strozzi and as a father, and they will listen to me. This evening I will invite the forty members of my family to supper; I will tell them what has happened to me. We shall see, we shall see! This is not the end. Let the Medicis look out for themselves! Farewell, I am going to the Pazzis; moreover, I was on my way there with Pierre when he was arrested.

LORENZO. There are many devils, Philippe; the one which is tempting you now is not the least of all to be feared.

PHILIPPE. What do you mean?

LORENZO. Beware of it; it is a demon more beautiful than Apollo—liberty, patriotism, men's happiness, all these words vibrate like harp-strings at its approach; it is the sound of the silver scales of its flaming wings. The tears of its eyes fertilize the earth, and it holds the palm of martyrs in its hand. Its words purify the air about its lips; its flight is so rapid that none can say where it goes. Beware of it! Once in my life I saw it cross the heavens. I was bending over my books; the touch of its hand stirred my hair like a light plume. Whether I listened or not, we will not say.

PHILIPPE. I understand you only with difficulty, and I know not why I am afraid of understanding you.

LORENZO. Have you only this thought in your head: to deliver your sons? Place your finger upon your conscience; does not another thought, more vast, more terrible, impel you like an overwhelming chariot into the midst of those young men?

PHILIPPE. Well, yes; may the injustice done to my family be the signal of liberty. For myself, and for all, I am going!

LORENZO. Beware of yourself, Philippe; you have thought of the welfare of humanity.

PHILIPPE. What does that mean? Are you an infectious vapor within as without? You who have talked to me of a precious liquor of which you were the flagon, is that what you enclose!

LORENZO. I am indeed precious to you, for I shall slay Alexander.

PHILIPPE. You?

LORENZO. I, to-morrow or the day after. Go home, try to deliver your children; if you can not, let them submit to a light punishment; I know pertinently that there is no other danger for them, and I repeat to you that in a few days from now there will be no more of an Alexander de Medicis in Florence than there is here a sun at midnight.

PHILIPPE. When that is accomplished, why should I be wrong to think of liberty? Will it not come when you have committed your deed, if you do commit it?

LORENZO. Philippe, Philippe, beware of yourself! You have sixty years of virtue over your gray head; it is too valuable a stake at hazard in a game of dice.

PHILIPPE. If you are hiding beneath these somber words something that I should hear, speak; you irritate me strangely.

LORENZO. Such as you see me, Philippe, I was once virtuous. I believed in virtue, in human grandeur, as a martyr believes in God. I have shed more tears over poor Italy than Niobe over her children.

PHILIPPE. Well, Lorenzo?

LORENZO. My youth was as pure as gold. During twenty years of silence the thunderbolt was gathering in my breast; and I must be in reality the spark of a thunderbolt, for suddenly, a certain night as I was sitting in the ruins of the colosseum, I know not why, I arose; I stretched my young arms to heaven, and I swore that one of the tyrants of my country should die by my hand. I was a peaceful student, and at that time I was occupied only with art and science, and it is impossible for me to say how that strange oath developed in me. Perhaps that is what a man feels when he falls in love.

PHILIPPE. I have always had confidence in you, and yet I believe I am dreaming.

LORENZO. And I also. I was happy then; my heart and hands were at peace; I was entitled to the throne, and I had but to let the sun rise and set, to see blossom around me every human hope. Men had influenced me neither for good nor evil; but I was good, and, to my everlasting misfortune, I wished to be great. I must confess, if Providence forced me to the resolution of killing a tyrant, whoever he may be, pride forced me to it also. What more can I say to you? All the Caesars of the world reminded me of Brutus.

PHILIPPE. The pride of virtue is a noble pride. Why do you defend yourself against it?

LORENZO. You will never know, short of madness, the nature of the thought which has agitated me. To comprehend the feverish exaltation which begot in me the Lorenzo who is speaking to you, it would be necessary for my heart and brains to be bared beneath the scalpel. A statue which should descend from its pedestal to walk in public places among men would perhaps be comparable to what I was the day I began to live with this idea: I must be a Brutus.

PHILIPPE. You astonish me more and more.

LORENZO. At first I wished to kill Clement VII. I was not able to do it because I was banished from Rome before the time. I renewed my task with Alexander. I wished to act alone, without the aid of any man. I was working for humanity; but my pride mingled with all my philanthropic dreams. It was necessary then to begin by stratagem a single combat with my enemy. I did not wish to arouse the masses, nor to conquer the garrulous glory of a paralytic like Cicero; I wished the man himself, to grapple hand to hand with living tyranny, to kill it, and afterward to carry my bloody sword to the rostrum and let the fumes of Alexander's blood mount to the nostrils of the haranguers, to revive the ardor of their sluggish brains.

PHILIPPE. What a will of iron you have, friend! What a will of iron!

LORENZO. The task which I imposed upon myself was difficult with Alexander. Florence was, like it is to-day, drowned in wine and blood. The Emperor and the Pope have made a duke of a butcher's boy. To please my cousin, it was necessary to reach him through the tears of families; to become his friend and gain his confidence, it was necessary to mingle in his drunken revelries. I was as pure as a lily, and yet I did not recoil before that task. Let us not speak of what I have become because of that. You can understand what I have suffered, and there are wounds upon which one does not raise the dressings with impunity. I have become vicious, cowardly, an object of opprobrium and shame; what does it matter? That is not the question.

PHILIPPE. You drop your head; your eyes are humid.

LORENZO. No, I am not blushing; plaster masks have no redness in the service of shame. I have done what I have done. You will only know that I have succeeded in my enterprise. Alexander will presently come into a certain place, whence he will not depart alive. I am at the end of my trouble, and you may be certain, Philippe, that the wild buffalo, when the herdsman strikes him to the ground, is not surrounded with more snares, with more running-knots, than I have woven around my bastard. That heart, to which an army could not have attained in a year, is now bared beneath my hand; I have only to let my stiletto fall in order to penetrate it. All will be done. Now, do you know what has happened to me, and that of which I wish to warn you?

PHILIPPE. You are our Brutus if you speak the truth.

LORENZO. I believe myself a Brutus, my poor Philippe; I remembered the golden baton covered with bark. Now, I am acquainted with men, and I advise you not to mingle with them.

PHILIPPE. Why?

LORENZO. Ah, you have lived alone, Philippe. Like a shining beacon you have remained motionless beside the ocean of men, and you have beheld in the waters the reflection of your own light; from the depths of your solitude you found the ocean magnificent beneath the splendid canopy of heaven; you did not count each wave, you did not hear the sound of it; you were full of confidence in God's handiwork. But I, during all this time, have dived; I have plunged into this rough sea of life; I have traversed all the depths of it, covered with my diving-bell; while you were admiring the surface, I saw the debris of shipwrecks, the bones and the leviathans.

PHILIPPE. Your sadness is heart-rending to me.

LORENZO. It is because I see you such as I was, and upon the point of doing that which I have done, that I talk to you thus. I do not despise men; the fault of books and of historians is that they show them different than they are. Life is like a city: one may remain in it for fifty or sixty years without seeing anything but promenades and palaces; but you must not go into the gambling-houses, nor stop on your way home at the windows of the poor neighborhoods. This is my advice, Philippe; if it is a question of saving your children, I tell you to keep quiet; it is the best means of having them returned to you after a slight reprimand. If it is a question of attempting anything for mankind, I advise you to cut off your arms, for you will not be long in discovering that you are the only one who has any.

PHILIPPE. I can conceive that the role you are playing has given you such ideas. If I understand you aright, you have taken a hideous route to a sublime end, and you believe that everything resembles that which you have seen.

LORENZO. I have awakened from my dreams, nothing more. I am telling you the danger of having them. I know life, and it is a sink-hole of corruption; be persuaded of that. Do not meddle with it if you respect anything.

PHILIPPE. Stop; do not break as a reed my staff of old age. I believe in all those things that you call dreams; I believe in virtue, modesty, and liberty.

LORENZO. You have not seen me, Lorenzaccio, in the street! And the children do not fling mud at me! The beds of young girls are still warm with my perspiration, and the fathers do not seize their knives and brooms to fell me as I pass! In the midst of these ten thousand homes which you behold, the seventh generation will still be talking of the night I entered there, and not one of them heaves out a plowman to split me in twain like a rotten log! The air which you breathe, Philippe, I am breathing, too; my robe of party-colored silk trails idly over the fine sand of the promenades; not one drop of poison falls into my cup; what am I saying? O, Philippe! the mothers of the poor shamelessly raise their daughters' veils when I pause upon their thresholds; they let me look upon their beauty, with a smile viler than the kiss of Judas, while I, pinching the chin of the maiden, clinch my fists in rage, as I rattle four or five paltry gold pieces in my pocket.

PHILIPPE. Let not the tempter despise the weak. Why tempt, if there is any doubt?

LORENZO. Am I a Satan? Light of Heaven! I remember yet, I should have wept with the first girl that I seduced, if she hadn't begun to laugh. When I began to play my role of modern Brutus, I walked in my new garb of the vast brotherhood of vice, like the tender child in the giant's armor of the fable. I believed that corruption was a stigma, and that only monsters bore the marks of it. I began by proclaiming that my twenty years of virtue was a suffocating mask. O, Philippe! then I entered upon the life, and I saw that at my approach every one met me half-way; all the masks fell before my gaze; humanity raised its veil and showed me, as to an adept worthy of it, its monstrous nudity. I saw men as they are, and I said to myself, "For what am I striving?" When I wandered about the streets of Florence, accompanied by my shadow, I looked around me, I sought for the faces which should give me courage, and I demanded of myself, "When I shall have done my deed, will that one profit by it? " I saw republicans in their studies; I entered into the shops; I watched and listened. I gathered the conversation of the masses; I noted the effect which tyranny produced upon them; I drank at patriotic banquets the wine which engenders the metaphor and the personification; I have swallowed, between two kisses, the most virtuous of tears; I was always watching for humanity to show me something of honesty upon its face. I observed as a lover observes his fiancée while waiting for the wedding-day.

PHILIPPE. If you have only seen the evil, I pity you; but I can not believe you. Evil exists, but not without the good, as the shadow exists, but not without the light.

LORENZO. You only see in me a despiser of men: that is an injustice to me. I know perfectly well that there are good ones among them; but what are they serving, what are they doing, how are they acting? Of what use is it that conscience be alive, if the arm is dead? From certain points of view everything becomes good; a dog is a faithful friend; one may find in him the best of servants, as one may also see that he wallows in corruption, and that the tongue which licks his master's hand, smells of the refuse of a neighborhood. All that I can see is that I am lost, and that men will not profit by it any more than they will understand me.

PHILIPPE. Poor child, this is heart-rending! But if you were virtuous, when you shall have delivered your country, you will become so again. That rejoices my old heart, Lorenzo, the thought that you are upright; so you will throw aside the hideous disguise which is disfiguring you, and you will become again as pure a metal as the bronze statues of Harmodius and Aristogeiton.

LORENZO. Philippe, Philippe, I have been virtuous. The hand which has once raised the veil of truth can never let it fall again; it rests immovable until death, always holding that terrible veil, and lifting it higher and higher above the head of the man, until the angel of death seals his eyes.

PHILIPPE. All maladies are curable; and vice is a malady also.

LORENZO. It is too late. I have trained myself to my calling. Vice used to be for me a garment; now it is incorporated into my being. I am truly a ruffian, and when I joke about my peers, I feel as serious as death in the midst of my gaiety. Brutus feigned insanity in order to kill Tarquin, and what surprises me in him is, that he did not lose his reason. Profit by my example, Philippe, that is what I have to say to you; do not work for your country.

PHILIPPE. If I believed you, it seems to me that the sky would be forever darkened, and that my old age would be condemned to grope its way. It may be true that you have taken a dangerous route; why should I not take some other, which would lead me to the same point? My purpose is to appeal to the people, and to act openly.

LORENZO. Beware, Philippe! he who tells you this knows whereof he speaks. Take whatever way you will, you will always have to deal with men.

PHILIPPE. I believe in the honesty of republicans.

LORENZO. I will make a wager with you. I am going to kill Alexander! Once my deed is accomplished, if the republicans deport themselves as they should, it will be easy for them to establish a republic the most beautiful that has ever blossomed upon earth. That they have the people with them, it is understood. I wager that neither they nor the people will do anything. All that I ask of you is not to get mixed up in it; speak, if you wish to, but weigh your words, and still more your actions. Leave me to accomplish my task. You have clean hands, and I have nothing to lose.

PHILIPPE. Do it, and you will see.

LORENZO. So be it; but remember this. Do you see, in that small house, that family assent bled around a table? Would you not take them for men? They have a body, and a mind within the body. Nevertheless, if I should be seized with a desire to enter their home, all alone, as you see me, and to stab their oldest son in their very midst, there would not a knife be raised against me.

PHILIPPE. You horrify me! How can the heart remain pure with hands like yours?

LORENZO. Come, go home to your palace, and strive to deliver your children.

PHILIPPE. But why will you kill the Duke, if you have such ideas?

LORENZO. Why? You ask that?

PHILIPPE. If you believe that it is a murder useless to your country, why do you commit it?

LORENZO. You ask me that to my face? Just look at me. I used to be handsome, happy, and virtuous.

PHILIPPE. What an abyss—what an abyss you open to me!

LORENZO. You demand of me why I kill Alexander? Do you wish me to poison myself, or jump into the Arno? Do you wish me to become a specter, and that in striking upon this skeleton, no *(He strikes his breast.)* sound should arise? If I am but a shadow of myself, would you have me tear away the only thread that binds my heart to my life of former days? Do you consider that this murder is all that remains to me of my virtue? Do you consider that I have been slipping for two years upon a perpendicular wall, and that the murder is the only straw that I have been able to grasp? Do you think that I have no more pride, because I have no more shame? And would you have me allow the enigma of my life to die in silence? Yes, this is certain; if I could become virtuous again, if my apprenticeship to vice could be blotted out, I perhaps would spare that cattle-driver. But I love wine, women, and song; do you understand that? If you honor anything in me, it is this murder which you honor, perhaps, just because you would not commit it yourself! Long enough have my ears been tingling, and the execrations of men have poisoned the bread I eat; I am tired of hearing men's gossip bawled to the four winds of heaven; the world must know just who I am, and who he is. Thank God! I will, perhaps, kill Alexander to-morrow—in two days at the most. Those who hover around me with suspicious eyes, as around some monstrous curiosity from America, will be able to get their fill and exhaust themselves of words. Whether men understand me or not, whether they act or not, I shall have said all that I have to say; I shall make them open their lips, if I do not make them scour their weapons, and humanity will preserve upon its cheek the slap of my sword, branded in characters of blood. Let them call me whatever they will, Brutus or Eratostratus, I do not wish them to forget me. My entire life is at the end of my dagger, and whether Providence turn the head or not upon hearing me strike, I cast human nature head or tail upon the tomb of Alexander; in two days men will appear before the tribunal of my will.

PHILIPPE. All that astonishes me, and there are things in all that you have told me that pain me, and others that please me. But Pierre and Thomas are in prison, and I could not trust any one but myself with that affair. My anger would fret itself in vain; my feelings are too keenly aroused; you may be right, but I must do something. I am going to assemble my friends.

LORENZO. As you wish; but beware of yourself. Keep my secret, even from your friends; that is all that I ask of you.

(Exeunt.)

SCENE IV

(At the Soderini palace. Enter Catherine reading a note).

CATHERINE. "Lorenzo must have spoken to you of me; but who could talk to you worthily of a love like mine? Let my pen acquaint you with what my lips can not tell you, and what my heart wishes to sign with its blood. Alexander de Medicis."... If this were not addressed to me, I should think that the messenger had made a mistake, and what I read makes me doubt my eyes.

(Enter Marie.)

CATHERINE. Oh, my dear mother! see what somebody has written me; explain to me, if you can, this mystery.
MARIE. Unfortunate girl—unfortunate girl! He loves you? Where has he seen you? Where have you spoken with him?

CATHERINE. Nowhere; a messenger handed me this as I was leaving the church.

MARIE. Lorenzo, he says, must have spoken to you? Ah, Catherine, to have such a son as that! Yes, to make his mother's sister the mistress of the Duke, not even the mistress, oh, my daughter! What names do those creatures bear! I can not say; he wanted that of Lorenzo. Come, I wish to confront him with this open letter, and know, before God, what he will say to it.

CATHERINE. I thought that the Duke was in love... pardon, mother, but I thought that the Duke was in love with the Marquise of Cibo. Somebody told me so.

MARIE. It is true that he did love her, if he is capable of loving.

CATHERINE. He no longer loves her? Ah, how can one shamelessly offer a heart like that? Come, mother, come to see Lorenzo.

MARIE. Give me your arm. I don't know what is the matter with me for a few days; I have had fever every night; indeed, for three months it has scarcely left me. I have suffered too much, my poor Catherine; why did you read me that letter? I can bear no more. I am no longer young, and yet it seems to me that I could become so again under certain conditions; but all that I see allures me toward the tomb. Come, support me, poor child! I shall not trouble you for long.

(Exeunt.)

SCENE V

(The Marquis of Cibo's Palace.)

THE MARQUISE *(dressed, before a mirror).* When I think of this, it surprises me. What a precipice is life! Why, it is already nine o'clock, and it is the Duke whom I attend in this toilet! Let what will come of it, I wish to try my power.

(Enter the Cardinal.)

THE CARDINAL. What a beautiful costume, Marquise! How fragrant these flowers are!

THE MARQUISE. I can not receive you, Cardinal; I am expecting a friend. You will excuse me.

THE CARDINAL. I leave you—I leave you. That boudoir, the door of which I see is ajar, is a little paradise. Shall I wait for you there?

THE MARQUISE. I am in a hurry—pardon me. No, not in my boudoir; where you wish.

THE CARDINAL. I will return at a more favorable time. *(Exit.)*

THE MARQUISE. Why always the face of that priest? What circles that bald-headed vulture is describing around me, that I always find him behind me whenever I turn around? Can it be that my last hour is near.

(A page enters, who whispers to her).

THE MARQUISE. Very well, I am coming. Ah, this calling of a servant, you were not made for that, poor proud heart! *(Exit.)*

SCENE VI

(The Boudoir of the Marquise. The Marquise; the Duke.)

THE MARQUISE. That is my way of thinking; I would love you in that way.

THE DUKE. Words, words, and nothing more.

THE MARQUISE. You men, that is so little for you! To sacrifice the peace of her days, the sacred chastity of honor, even her children sometimes; only to live for one sole being in the world; to give herself away, in short, is all this to be called thus! But this is not worth while; what is the use of listening to a woman? A woman who talks of anything but dress and debauchery can not be imagined.

THE DUKE. You are dreaming wide awake.

THE MARQUISE. Yes, by heavens! yes, I have been dreaming. Alas! kings alone never do that; all the idle fancies of their caprice are transformed into realities, and even their nightmares are changed into marble. Alexander! Alexander! what does this mean? "I can, if I wish!" Ah, God himself no longer knows; before that phrase, the hands of peoples join in anxious prayer, and the pale herd of men holds its breath to listen.

THE DUKE. Let us say no more about that, my dear; it is tiresome.

THE MARQUISE. To be a king! do you know what it means? To have armies at command! To be the ray of sunlight which dries men's tears! To be both joy and sorrow! Ah, how that makes one shudder! How that old man of the Vatican would tremble if you were to spread your wings, my eaglet! The Emperor is so far away! The garrison is so devoted to you! And, moreover, an army may be disposed of, but not a whole people. The day when you shall have rallied the whole nation to you, when you shall be the leader of a free people, when you can say, "As the Doge of Venice weds the Adriatic, so I place the golden circlet upon the finger of my beautiful Florence, and her children are my children"... Ah! do you know what it is to have a nation take its benefactor in its arms? Do you know what it is to be borne like a cherished nursling by the vast ocean of men? Do you know what it is to be pointed out by a father to his son?

THE DUKE. All I care about is the taxes; provided they pay them, what is that to me?

THE MARQUISE. But at last somebody will assassinate you. The very stones of the earth will rise up to crush you. Ah, posterity! Have you never seen that specter beside your bed? Have you never asked yourself what generations unborn will think of you? And you are alive; there is still time. You have only to say the word. Are you unmindful of the future of the country? It is easy to be great when one is a king. Declare Florence independent; demand the execution of the treaty with the empire; draw your sword and show it; they will tell you to return it to its scabbard, that its flashes dazzle their eyes. Think how young you are! Nothing is yet settled on your account. The hearts of the people are very indulgent to princes, and public recognition is a profound depth of oblivion for past faults. You have had poor advice; you have been deceived. But there is still time; you have only to speak; so long as you are alive, the page is not turned in the book of doom.

THE DUKE. Enough, my dear, enough!

THE MARQUISE. Ah, when it is! When some miserable gardener, working by the day, comes reluctantly to water a few sickly daisies around the tomb of Alexander; when the poor breathe joyously the air of heaven, and no longer see soaring there the somber meteor of your power; when they speak of you with a shake of the head; when they number your grave among those of their fathers, are you sure that your last sleep will be a peaceful one? You who never go to mass, and care only for taxes, are you sure that eternity is deaf and that there is no echo of life in the hideous abode of the dead? Do you know where the tears of the people go to when the wind wafts them away?

THE DUKE. You have a pretty leg.

THE MARQUISE. Listen to me; you are thoughtless, I know, but you are not wicked; no, above all things you are not that—you could not be that. Come, arouse yourself; reflect a moment, only a moment, upon what I am saying to you. Is there nothing in it all? Am I indeed mad?

THE DUKE. All that is beyond my comprehension; but what do I do that is so bad? I am as good as my neighbors; I am as good as indeed, better than the Pope. You remind me of the Strozzis with all your talk; and you know that I detest them. You wish me to revolt against the Emperor; the Emperor is my stepfather, my dear friend. You imagine that the Florentines do not love me. I am sure that they do love me. Ah, zounds! if you should be right, what should I fear?

THE MARQUISE. You are not afraid of your people, but you are afraid of the Emperor; you have slain or dishonored hundreds of citizens, and you think you have taken every precaution when you wear a coat of mail under your coat.

THE DUKE. Hush! none of that.

THE MARQUISE. Ah! I am too impulsive; I say things that I ought not to say. My dear, who does not know that you are brave? You are as brave as you are handsome; whatever wrong you have done has been due to your youth, your head; what do I know about it? It is the blood which courses madly in your burning veins, the suffocating sun which weighs upon us. I beg of you that I may not be irrevocably lost; that my name, that my poor love for you, be not inscribed upon a list of infamy. I am a woman, it is true, and if beauty is everything to women, many others are better than I. But have you nothing—tell me, tell me now—come! have you nothing there! *(She strikes him over his head.)*

THE DUKE. What a demon! Sit down there, my darling.

THE MARQUISE. Ah, well; yes, I must confess it—yes, I am ambitious, not for myself, but for you—you and my dear Florence! O, God! you are witness of my suffering.

THE DUKE. You suffer! What is the matter with you?

THE MARQUISE. No, I do not suffer. Listen! listen! I see that you are getting weary with me. You count the moments, you turn your head. Do not go yet: it is perhaps the last time that I shall see you. Listen! I tell you that Florence calls you her new pestilence, and that there is not a cottage where your picture is not pasted upon the wall, with a thrust of a knife through the heart. If I am mad, if you should hate me to-morrow, what does it matter to me? You shall know that!

THE DUKE. Woe to you, if you play with my anger!

THE MARQUISE. Yes, woe to me! woe to me!

THE DUKE. Another time—to-morrow morning, if you wish—we will see each other again and talk of that. Do not be angry if I leave you now; I must go to the chase.

THE MARQUISE. Yes, woe to me! woe to me!

THE DUKE. Why? You are as solemn as a judge. Why the deuce, therefore, do you meddle with politics? Come, come! your little rôle of woman, and of true woman, is so becoming to you! You are too devout; that will improve. Help me put on my coat; my breast is quite bare.

THE MARQUISE. Good-by, Alexander.

(The Duke kisses her. Enter Cardinal Cibo.)

THE CARDINAL. Ah!—Excuse me, my Lord; I thought my sister was alone. I am very awkward; the penalty is mine. I beg your pardon.

THE DUKE. What do you mean by this? Come, Malaspina, this is what smacks of the priest. Ought you to see these things? Come along—come along! What the devil is it to you?

(Exeunt together.)

THE MARQUISE *(alone, looking at a picture of her husband).* Where are you now, Laurent? It is past noon; you are walking on the terrace, before the great chestnut-trees. Your sleek heifers are grazing around you; your farm-hands are eating their dinner in the shade; the lawn spreads its pale mantle to the rays of the sun; the trees, preserved by your care, are murmuring religiously above the head of their old master, while the echo of our long piazzas respectfully repeat the sound of your light footsteps. Oh, my Laurent! I have lost the treasure of your honor; I have devoted to ridicule and doubt the last years of your noble life; you will never again press to you bosom a heart that is worthy of yours; it will be a trembling hand which will bring you your evening meal when you return from the chase. *(Exit.)*

SCENE VII

(At the Strozzi Palace. The Forty Strozzis, at supper.)

PHILIPPE. My children, be seated at the table.

THE GUESTS. Why are there two empty seats?

PHILIPPE. PIERRE and Thomas are in jail.

THE GUESTS. For what reason?

PHILIPPE. Because Salviati insulted my daughter, whom you see, at the fair at Mount Olivet, in public, and before her brother Leon.

Pierre and Thomas have killed Salviati, and Alexander de Medicis has had them arrested to revenge the death of his ruffian.

THE GUESTS. Death to the Medicis!

PHILIPPE. I have gathered my family together to relate to them my sorrows, and beg them to assist me. Let us eat our supper, and afterward go with sword in hand to demand my two sons, if you have a mind to do so.

THE GUESTS. It is agreed. We are willing.

PHILIPPE. It is time for this to end, you know. They would kill our sons and dishonor our daughters. It is time for Florence to teach these bastards what the right over life and death means. The Eight have no right to condemn my children; and I would never survive it, you know!

THE GUESTS. Have no fear, Philippe; we are here.

PHILIPPE. I am the head of the family: how could I bear for any one to insult me? There are quite as many of us as of the Medicis, as many of the Ruccellai, the Aldobrandini, and twenty other families. Why should they have the power to destroy our children rather than we theirs? Let somebody but light a keg of powder under the walls of the citadel, and put the German garrison to rout. What is left to the Medicis? There lies their strength; aside from that they are nothing. Are we men? Shall it be said that Florentine families are struck down with a blow of an ax, and that people tear from native soil roots as old as the soil itself? They have begun with us, we must stand firm; our first cry of alarm, like the whistle of a bird-catcher, will call together over Florence a whole army of eagles driven from their nest; they are not far away; they are circling about the city, their eyes fixed upon its belfry towers. We will plant upon them the black banner of pestilence; they will flock together at that signal of death. These are the colors of celestial anger. To-night let us first go to deliver our sons; to-morrow we will go together, with naked swords, to the doors of all the great families; there are more than fourscore palaces in Florence, and from each one of them a band like ours will come out when liberty knocks at the door.

THE GUESTS. Long live liberty!

PHILIPPE. God is my witness that violence has forced me to draw the sword; that for sixty years I have been a good and peaceful citizen; that I have never injured anybody in the world, and that half of my fortune has been used to succor the unfortunate.

THE GUESTS. That is true.

PHILIPPE. It is a just vengeance that drives me to revolt, and I become a rebel because God made me a father. I am actuated by no ambitious motive, either of interest or of pride. My cause is loyal, honorable, and sacred. Fill your glasses and rise. Our vengeance is an offering that we can break without fear and share before God. I drink to the death of the Medicis!

THE GUESTS *(rising and drinking).* To the death of the Medicis!

LOUISE *(setting down her glass).* Ah, I am dying!

PHILIPPE. What is the matter, my daughter, my darling child? What is the matter? My God! what has happened? My God! my God, how pale you are! Speak—What is the matter with you? Speak to your father. Help! help!—a doctor! Quick! quick! there's no time to lose!

LOUISE. I am dying I am dying! *(She dies.)*

PHILIPPE. She is going, my friends—she is going! A doctor! My daughter is poisoned! *(He drops upon his knees beside Louise.)*

A GUEST. Cut her corset! make her drink some tepid water. If it is poison, tepid water is what she needs.

(The servants run in.)

ANOTHER GUEST. Slap her hands; open the windows, and slap her hands.

ANOTHER GUEST. Perhaps it is only a dizziness; she may have drunk too fast.

ANOTHER GUEST. Poor child! how calm her features are! She can not be dead so suddenly as all that.

PHILIPPE. My child, are you dead—are you dead, Louise, my darling daughter?

THE FIRST GUEST. Here comes the doctor.

(A doctor enters.)

THE SECOND GUEST. Hurry, sir! tell us if it is poison.

PHILIPPE. It is a faint, is it not?

THE DOCTOR. Poor girl! She is dead.

(A profound silence reigns in the room; Philippe continues kneeling beside Louise, holding her hands.)

A GUEST. It is the poison of the Medicis. We must not leave Philippe in that condition. That immobility is frightful!

ANOTHER GUEST. I am sure I am not mistaken. There was a servant around the table who used to be employed by Salviati's wife.

ANOTHER GUEST. It was he that did it, without any doubt. Let us go and arrest him.

(Exeunt.)

FIRST GUEST. Philippe does not reply to anything that is said to him; he is overwhelmed by the blow.

ANOTHER GUEST. It is horrible! It is a most unheard-of murder!

ANOTHER GUEST. It cries vengeance to high Heaven. Let us go and kill Alexander.

ANOTHER GUEST. Yes, let us go. Death to Alexander! It is he that ordered it done. Fools that we are! His hatred of us is not a thing of yesterday. We are acting too late.

ANOTHER GUEST. Salviati did not want anything of that poor Louise on his own account; he was acting for The Duke. Come, let us be off, though they should kill us to the very last man.

PHILIPPE *(arising).* My friends, you will bury my poor girl, will you not *(He puts on his cloak.)*, in my garden, behind the fig-trees? Farewell, my dear friends, farewell. Take care of yourselves.

A GUEST. Where are you going, Philippe?

PHILIPPE. I have borne enough, you know! I have borne all that I can bear. My two sons are in jail, and now my daughter is dead. I can bear no more; I am going away.

A GUEST. You are going away? Going away without revenge?

PHILIPPE. Yes, yes. Only shroud my poor girl; do not bury her; I will attend to that; I will do it in my own way, with the assistance of some poor monks whom I know, and who will come for her to-morrow. What is the use of looking at her? She is dead; therefore it is of no use. Farewell, my friends. Go home; take care of yourselves.

A GUEST. Do not let him go; he is out of his mind.

ANOTHER GUEST. How terrible! I feel ready to faint in this room. *(Exit.)*

PHILIPPE. Do not do violence to me; do not lock me up in a chamber with my dead child. Let me go.

A GUEST. Avenge yourself, Philippe. Allow us to avenge you. Let your Louise be our Lucretia! We will make Alexander drink the rest of his glass.

ANOTHER GUEST. A new Lucretia! We will take an oath over her body to die for liberty! Go to your room, Philippe; think of your country. Do not retract what you have said.

PHILIPPE. Liberty—revenge you know that is all very fine. I have two sons in jail, and here is my daughter dead. If I stay here, everybody about me will die. The important point is for me to go away and for you to keep quiet. When my door and my windows are closed, no one will think any more about the Strozzis. If they remain open, I shall see you all fall one after the other. I am old, you know; it is time for me to shut up shop. Farewell, my friends; keep quiet. If I am no longer here, they will do nothing to you. I am going to Venice.

A GUEST. It is storming frightfully: stay here to-night.

PHILIPPE. Do not bury my poor child; my old monks will come to-morrow and take her away. God of justice! God of justice! how have I offended you? *(He runs off.)*

ACT THE FOURTH

SCENE I

(At the Palace of the Duke. Enter the Duke and Lorenzo.)

THE DUKE. I should like to have been there; there must have been more than one angry face there. But I can not imagine who poisoned that Louise.

LORENZO. Nor I either—unless it was you.

THE DUKE. Philippe must be furious! They say that he has gone to Venice. Thank God, I am rid of that insupportable old man! As for the dear family, they will be good enough to keep quiet. Do you know that they have very nearly stirred up a little insurrection in their neighborhood? Somebody has killed two Germans.

LORENZO. What I am most sorry about is that that good Salviati has a leg amputated. Have you found your coat of mail yet?

THE DUKE. No, indeed; I am more displeased about it than I can say.

LORENZO. Mistrust Giomo; it was he that stole it from you. What do you wear in place of it?

THE DUKE. Nothing; I can not bear any other; there are no others as light as that.

LORENZO. That is unfortunate for you.

THE DUKE. You have said nothing to me about your aunt.

LORENZO. It was from forgetfulness, for she adores you. Her eyes have lost their rest since the star of your love has arisen in her poor heart. I pray you, my Lord, have some pity upon her; say when you wish to receive her, and at what hour it will be allowable for her to sacrifice the little virtue that she has to you.

THE DUKE. Are you talking seriously?

LORENZO. As seriously as death itself. I should like to see that an aunt of mine did not flirt with you!

THE DUKE. Where can I see her?

LORENZO. In my chamber, my Lord. I will have white curtains put to my bed and a pot of mignonette upon the table; after which I will write down in your note-book that my aunt will be in dishabille at midnight precisely, in order that you may not forget her after supper.

THE DUKE. I will take good care of that. Pest! Catherine is a morsel fit for a king. Ah, tell me, clever boy, are you sure that she will come? How did you accomplish it?

LORENZO. I will not tell you that.

THE DUKE. I am going to look at a horse which I have just bought. Good-by until evening. Come for me after supper; we will go together to your house. As for the Cibo, I am tired to death of her. Yesterday again I had to entertain her during the entire chase. Good afternoon, my dear boy. *(Exit.)*

LORENZO *(alone).* So it is settled. This evening I will take him home with me, and to-morrow the republicans will see what they have to do, for the Duke of Florence will be dead. I must apprise Scoronconcolo. Hasten, sun, if you are curious about the news that this night will bring forth. *(Exit.)*

SCENE II

(A street. Pierre and Thomas Strozzi, leaving the jail.)

PIERRE. I was sure that the Eight would absolve me, and you also. Come, let us knock at our door, and go to find father. That is strange; the shutters are closed.

THE DOORKEEPER *(opening the door).* Alas! my Lords, do you know the news?

PIERRE. What news? You look like a ghost from some tomb, at the door of this deserted palace.

THE DOORKEEPER. Is it possible that you know nothing?

(Two monks arrive.)

THOMAS. What could we know? We are just out of jail. Speak; what has happened?

THE DOORKEEPER. Alas! my poor young masters, it is horrible to relate!

THE MONKS *(drawing near).* Is this the Strozzi palace?

THE DOORKEEPER. Yes; what do you wish?

THE MONKS. We have come for the body of Louise Strozzi. Here is Philippe's authorization, in order that you should allow us to take it away.

PIERRE. What are you saying? Whose body are you asking for?

THE MONKS. Keep out of the way, my child; you bear a resemblance to Philippe upon your face. There is nothing good for you to learn here.

THOMAS. What? She is dead! Dead! God of heaven! *(He takes a seat at one side.)*

PIERRE. I am stronger than you think. Who killed my sister? for one does not die at her age in the space of a single night, without adequate cause. Who killed her, that I may kill him? Answer me, or you are dead yourself.

THE DOORKEEPER. Alas! alas! who can say? Nobody knows.

PIERRE. Where is my father? Come, Thomas, no tears. By Heaven! my heart feels as though it were turning to stone in my bosom, and would remain a stone throughout eternity.

THE MONKS. If you are Philippe's son, come with us; we will take you to him. He has been at our convent since yesterday.

PIERRE. And I do not know who killed my sister! Listen to me, priests; if you are in the image of God, you can receive an oath. By all the instruments of torture under heaven, by all the tortures of hell... No, I do not wish to say a word. Let us hurry, that I may see my father. O, God! O, God! grant that my suspicions be true, in order that I may grind them beneath my heel like grains of sand. Come, come, before I lose my strength. Do not say a word; it is a question of vengeance, you know, such as celestial anger never dreamed of.

(Exeunt.)

SCENE III

(A street. Lorenzo, Scoronconcolo.)

LORENZO. Go home, and do not fail to come at midnight; you will shut yourself into my study until some one comes to warn you.

SCORONCONCOLO. Yes, my Lord. *(Exit.)*

LORENZO *(alone)*. Of what tiger was my mother dreaming when she was with child with me? When I think that I used to love flowers, meadows, and the sonnets of Petrarch, the specter of my youth rises up before me with a shudder... God! why does the little phrase, "Until this evening," make this burning joy penetrate to my very marrow like a red-hot iron? From what tawny breast, from what hairy embraces, did I spring? What has that man done to me? When I put my ringer on it and reflect who will hear me say to-morrow, "I have killed him," without replying, "Why did you kill him?" That is strange. He has injured others, but he has been kind to me, at least in his own fashion. If I had only remained quietly in the depths of my solitudes at Cafaggiuolo, he would not have come to seek me there, and I came to seek him at Florence. For what reason? Did the specter of my father lead me, like Orestes, toward a new.Ægisthus? Has he then offended me? It is strange, and yet I have sacrificed everything for this act; the sole thought of this murder has caused the dreams of my life to crumble to dust; I have been nothing but a ruin since this crime, like a sinister raven, alighted upon my path and beckoned to me. What does it mean? Just now, in crossing the square, I heard two men talking of a comet. Are these the beatings of a human heart that I feel within the walls of my chest? Ah, why does this idea come to me so often of late—"Am I following the will of God?" Is there a cloud over my head? When I enter into that chamber, and wish to draw my sword from its scabbard, I am afraid of drawing the flaming sword of the archangel, and then of falling in ashes upon my prey. *(Exit.)*

SCENE IV

(The Marquis of Cibo's house. Enter the Cardinal and the Marquise.)

THE MARQUISE. As you like, Malaspina.

THE CARDINAL. Yes, as I like. Think twice, Marquise, before trifling with me. Are you like other women, and a man must have a gold chain around his neck and a mandate in his hand for you to comprehend who he is? Are you waiting until a valet shouts at the top of his voice upon opening a door before me, to know what my power is? Mark this: it is not the title that makes a man. I am neither an envoy of the Pope nor a captain of Charles V; I am more than that.

THE MARQUISE. Yes, I know that. The Emperor of Rome has sold his shadow to the devil: that imperial shadow wanders about, tricked out in a red robe, under the name of Cibo.

THE CARDINAL You are Alexander's mistress; think of that; and your secret is in my hands.

THE MARQUISE. Do whatever you please with it; we will see what use a confessor knows how to make of his conscience.

THE CARDINAL. You are mistaken. It was not by your confession that I learned it; I discovered it with my own eyes; I saw you kissing The Duke. You would have admitted to me in the confessional that I could speak of it without a breach of confidence, since I saw it outside of the confessional.

THE MARQUISE. Well, then, what next?

THE CARDINAL. Why did the Duke leave you with such a nonchalant air, and sighing like a school-boy when the bell rings? You have surfeited him with your patriotism, which, like an insipid beverage, mingles with all the dishes of your table. What books have you read, and what foolish duenna was your governess, that you should not know that a king's mistress ordinarily talks of other things than patriotism?

THE MARQUISE. I confess that no one ever taught me very clearly what a king's mistress should talk about. I neglected to inform myself upon that point, as also, perhaps, to eat rice to fatten myself, after the fashion of the Turk.

THE CARDINAL. No great learning is required to keep a lover a little longer than three days.

THE MARQUISE. It would have been very easy for a priest to teach a woman that; why didn't you advise me?

THE CARDINAL. Do you wish me to advise you? Put on your cloak, and go and slip into the Duke's alcove. If he expects patriotic talk upon seeing you, prove to him that you do not talk that way at all times; be like a somnambulist, and conduct yourself in such a manner as to convince him that if he were to fall asleep upon your republican heart, it would not be from weariness. Are you a virgin? Is there no more wine of Cyprus? Have you not in the depths of your memory some joyous song? Have you not read Aretino?

THE MARQUISE. O, heavens! I have heard such words as those murmured into the ears of the hideous old women in the market-place. If you are not a priest, are you a man? Are you sure that there is not a God in heaven, that you thus put your purple itself to the blush?

THE CARDINAL. There is nothing in the world so virtuous as the ear of a depraved woman. Pretend to understand me or not, but remember that my brother is your husband.

THE MARQUISE. What interest you can have in torturing me so is what I can understand but vaguely. You inspire me with horror. What do you want of me?

THE CARDINAL. There are secrets that a woman ought not to know, but that she can make prosper by knowing their elements.

THE MARQUISE. What mysterious thread of your somber thoughts would you like to make me grasp? If your desires are as terrifying as your threats, speak; show me at least the hair which suspends the sword over my head.

THE CARDINAL. I can speak only in ambiguous terms, for the reason that I am not sure of you. Let it suffice for you to know, that if you had been another woman you would be a queen by this time. Since you call me the Emperor's shadow, you would have perceived that it is large enough to intercept the sun of Florence. Do you know where a woman's smile can lead? Do you know to what fortunes founded in the alcoves attain? Alexander is the son of a pope, understand that; and when that pope was at Bologna... But I am going too far.

THE MARQUISE. Beware of confessing in your turn. If you are my husband's brother, I am Alexander's mistress.

THE CARDINAL. You have been that, Marquise, and many others also.

THE MARQUISE. I have been that; yes, thank God! I have been that.

THE CARDINAL. I was sure that you would begin with your dreams; it will be necessary, however, some day to come to mine. Listen to me; we are quarreling to no purpose. Seek a reconciliation with Alexander, and although I offended you just now by telling you how, I can only repeat what I said. Allow yourself to be guided; in a year, in two years, you would thank me. I have struggled a long time to become what I am, and I know how far one may go. If I were sure of you, I would tell you things that God himself will never know.

THE MARQUISE. Hope for nothing, and be assured of my contempt. *(She starts to go.)*

THE CARDINAL. One moment! Not so fast! Do you not hear the sound of horses' feet? Should not my brother come to-day or to-morrow? Do you know me for a man of two sides? Go to the palace this evening, or you are lost.

THE MARQUISE. In short, that you may be ambitious, that all means may be fair to you, I can conceive; but will you speak more clearly? Come, Malaspina, I do not wish to despair completely because of my perversion. If you can convince me, do so; speak frankly. What is your aim?

THE CARDINAL. You do not despair of being convinced; is it not so? Do you take me for a child, and think that it is only necessary to rub my lips with honey to make me open them? Act first; I will talk to you afterward. The day when, as a woman, you shall have gained the necessary control, not over the mind of Alexander, Duke of Florence, but over the heart of Alexander, your lover, I will teach you the rest, and you will know what I expect.

THE MARQUISE. And so, when I have read Aretino to give me my first experience, I shall have to read the secret book of your thoughts in order to acquire a second? Do you wish me to tell you what you do not dare to tell me? You will serve the Pope until the Emperor finds that you are a better valet than the Pope himself. You hope that some day the Emperor will owe to you, very truly, very completely, the enslavement of Italy, and that day—oh! that day, is it not true?— he who is king of half the earth would be very well able to give you the paltry inheritance of heaven in recompense. To govern Florence by governing the Duke, you would make a tool of a woman, if you could. When poor Ricciardi Cibo shall have made two or three *coups d'etat* with Alexander, it will presently be said that Ricciardi Cibo leads the Duke, and the woman is led by her brother-in-law; and as you say, who knows just where the tears of the people, become a flood, might launch your bark? Is it not something like that? Of course my imagination is unable to go as far as yours; but I believe it is pretty much like that.

THE CARDINAL. Go this evening to the Duke, or you are lost.

THE MARQUISE. Lost? How so?

THE CARDINAL. Your husband shall know all.

THE MARQUISE. Let him, let him; I will kill myself.

THE CARDINAL A woman's threat! Listen, and do not trifle with me. Whether you have comprehended me well or not, go this evening to The Duke.

THE MARQUISE. No.

THE CARDINAL. There is your husband coming into the courtyard. By all that is good and holy in the world, I will tell him everything if you say no again.

THE MARQUISE. No, no, no!

(Enter the Marquis.)

THE MARQUISE. Laurent, while you were at Massa I devoted myself to Alexander. I devoted myself to him, knowing what he was, and what a miserable role I was playing. But here is a priest who wishes to make me play one viler still; he proposes horrible things to me to secure me the title of mistress to the Duke, and turn it to his advantage. *(She throws herself upon her knees.)*

THE MARQUIS. Are you mad? What does she mean, Malaspina? How now! you look like a statue. Is this a comedy, Cardinal? Well, then, what am I to think of this?

THE CARDINAL. God bless my soul! *(Exit.)*

THE MARQUIS. She has fainted. Hallo! somebody bring some smelling-salts.

SCENE V

(Lorenzo's Chamber. Lorenzo. Two Servants.)

LORENZO. When you have placed those flowers upon the table and these at the foot of the bed, make a good fire, but for to-night see that it does not blaze, and that the coals give out heat without light. Give me the key, and go to bed.

(Enter Catherine.)

CATHERINE. Your mother is ill; won't you come to see her, Renzo?
LORENZO. My mother is ill?
CATHERINE. Alas! I must tell you the truth. I received a note from the Duke yesterday, in which he said that you had doubtless spoken to me of love in his behalf. The reading of that letter made Marie very ill.
LORENZO. I had not spoken of it, however. Could not you have told her that there was no truth in it?
CATHERINE. I did tell her so. Why is your chamber so fine and in such good order to-day? I did not know that a spirit of order was a strong point with you.
LORENZO. So the Duke has written you? It is strange that I did not know it. What do you think of his letter?
CATHERINE. What do I think of it?
LORENZO. Yes, of Alexander's declaration. What does your little innocent heart think of it?
CATHERINE. What would you have me think of it.
LORENZO. Were you not flattered? A love which excites the envy of so many women! Such a fine title to win, the mistress of... Go on, Catherine; tell my mother that I will follow you. Go away from here. Leave me!

(Exit Catherine.)

LORENZO. By heavens! what a man of wax I am! Is vice, like Dejanira's mantle, so deeply incorporated with the fibers of my being, that I can no longer be responsible for my tongue, and that the breath which leaves my lips is poisoned in spite of myself? I was going to corrupt Catherine; I believe I would corrupt my mother, if the idea were to seize me; for God only knows what bow the gods have bent inside my brain, and what force the arrows have which are shot forth from it. If all men are particles of an immense furnace, surely the unknown hand which fashioned me let fall a firebrand instead of a spark in this feeble, tottering frame of mine. I can deliberate and choose, but I can not retract when once I have chosen. O, God! do not young men of the time glory in vice, and have young men who leave college anything more urgent that self-perversion? What a slough must such specimens of humanity be, who rush thus into public-houses, with lips athirst for debauchery, when I, who only meant to assume their appearance, and entered evil places with a firm determination to remain pure beneath my semblance of sin, can neither recover myself nor wash my hands of it, even in blood! Poor Catherine! you would die nevertheless, like Louise Strozzi, or allow yourself to fall into the eternal abyss like so many others, if I were not here. O, Alexander! I am not religious, but I could wish that you might say your prayers before coming into this room to-night. Is not Catherine virtuous, irreproachable? For all that, how many words would it take to make that innocent dove the prey of that rough-haired gladiator? When I think that I came near speaking! How many girls, under their father's curse, are wandering about the confines of the city, or contemplating their close-shaven heads in the broken glass of some cell, who were just as good as Catherine, but who listened to a ruffian less clever than I! Ah, well; I have committed many crimes, and if my life is ever weighed in the balance of any judge whatever, there will be on the one side a mountain of sobs, but on the other there will perhaps be a drop of pure milk from Catherine's breast, which will have nourished legitimate children. *(Exit.)*

SCENE VI

(A valley; a convent and two monks; enter Phillppe Strozzi and two monks; some novitiates bearing the bier of Louise; they place it in a tomb.)

PHILIPPE. Let me kiss her before putting her in her last bed. When she had retired, it was thus that I bent over her to give her my goodnight kiss. Her melancholy eyes were half closed like this; but they would reopen like two azure flowers at the first ray of sunlight; she would arise softly, a smile upon her lips, and come to return to her old father his kiss of the evening before. Her celestial face used to make delightful an otherwise very sad moment, the awakening of a world-weary man. One day more, I would think, upon seeing the day break; one more furrow in my field. Then I would notice my daughter; life appeared to me in the form of her beauty, and the light of day was welcome.

(They close the tomb.)

PIERRE Strozzi *(behind the scenes)*. This way—come this way.

PHILIPPE. You will never more arise from your couch; never will you set your bare feet upon this turf to return to find your father. O, my Louise! God alone knew what you were to me; and I, I, I!

PIERRE *(entering)*. There are a hundred men at Sestino who have arrived from Piedmont. Come, Philippe; the time for tears is past.

PHILIPPE. Child, do you know what the time for tears is?

PIERRE. The exiles have assembled at Sestino; it is time to think of vengeance. Let us march boldly upon Florence with out little army. If we can arrive opportunely, in the night, and surprise the guards of the citadel, there's an end of it. By heavens! I will raise another monument than that to my sister.

PHILIPPE. Not I. Go without me, my friends.

PIERRE. We can not go without you; you know the confederates count upon your name. Francis I himself is expecting some move from you in the cause of liberty. He writes to you as to the leader of Florentine republicans; here is his letter.

PHILIPPE *(opening the letter)*. Tell him who brought this letter to say to the King of France that the day when Philippe takes up arms against his country he will have become a madman.

PIERRE. What is this new phrase?

PHILIPPE. The one that suits me.

PIERRE. Thus you will ruin the cause of the exiles, for the pleasure of making a set phrase? Beware, father; it is not a question of a passage from Pliny. Consider well before saying no.

PHILIPPE. I have known for sixty years what I ought to reply to that letter of the King of France.

PIERRE. This passes all comprehension! You will force me to say certain things to you... Come with us; father, I beg of you. When I was going to the Pazzis, did you not ask me to take you with me? Was the situation any different then?

PHILIPPE. Very different. An offended father who goes forth with sword in hand, in company with his friends, to demand justice, is very different from a rebel who arms himself against his country, in open campaign, and in contempt of law.

PIERRE. It was indeed a question of demanding justice! It was a question of overpowering Alexander! What change is there in the situation to-day? You do not love your country, or you would take advantage of an occasion like this.

PHILIPPE. An occasion! My God! this an occasion! *(He strikes the tomb.)*

PIERRE. Allow yourself to be persuaded.

PHILIPPE. I have not an ambitious sorrow. Leave me alone; I have said enough about it.

PIERRE. Obstinate old man, inexorable turner of phrases! you will be the cause of our ruin.

PHILIPPE. Shut up, insolent one! Get out of here!

PIERRE. I can not tell you my feelings. Go where you please; we will act without you this time. By the Eternal! it shall not be said that all is lost by fault of a translator of Latin. *(Exit.)*

PHILIPPE. Your day has come, Philippe! Everything indicates that your day has come. *(Exit.)*

SCENE VII

(A bank of the Arno; a quay. A long line of palaces is seen. Enter Lorenzo.)

LORENZO. The sun is setting; I have no time to lose, and yet everything here looks like lost time. *(He knocks at a door.)* Hallo, Signor Alamanno! hallo!

ALAMANNO *(upon his terrace)*. Who is there? What do you want of me?

LORENZO. I come to notify you that the Duke is to be killed to-night; take measures for to-morrow with your friends, if you love liberty?

ALAMANNO. By whom is Alexander to be killed?

LORENZO. By Lorenzo de Medicis.

ALAMANNO. Is that you, Lorenzaccio? Come in and take supper with some jolly fellows who are in my salon.

LORENZO. I have not time. Prepare to act to-morrow.

ALAMANNO. You wish to kill the Duke yourself? Go on! you have been drinking. *(Exit.)*

LORENZO *(alone)*. Perhaps I am wrong to tell them that it is I who will kill Alexander, for everybody refuses to believe me. *(He knocks at another door)*. Hallo, Signor Pazzi! hallo!

PAZZI *(upon his terrace)*. Who is calling me?

LORENZO. I have come to tell you that the Duke will be killed this night. Endeavor to act for the liberty of Florence to-morrow.

PAZZI. Who is going to kill the Duke?

LORENZO. No matter. Work away, you and your friends. I can not tell you the name of the man.

PAZZI. You are mad, imbecile! go to the devil! *(Exit.)*

LORENZO *(alone).* Evidently if I do not say that it is I, they will believe me still less. *(He knocks at a door.)* Hallo, Signor Corsini!

THE PURVEYOR *(upon his terrace).* What is it?

LORENZO. Duke Alexander will be killed tonight.

THE PURVEYOR. Indeed, Lorenzo! If you are drunk, go elsewhere with your jokes. You wounded a horse for me very untimely at the Nasi ball; may the devil take you! *(Exit.)*

LORENZO. Poor Florence! poor Florence! *(Exit.)*

SCENE VIII

(A plain. Enter Pierre Strozzi and two exiles.)

PIERRE. My father would not come. It was impossible for me to make him listen to reason.

FIRST EXILE. I will not announce that to my comrades; that would be enough to put them to rout.

PIERRE. Why so? Take your horse this evening; ride at full speed to Sestino; I will be there to-morrow morning. Say that Philippe has refused, but that Pierre does not refuse.

FIRST EXILE. The confederates want the name of Philippe; we can do nothing without that.

PIERRE. Philippe's surname is the same as mine; say that Strozzi will come; that will answer.

FIRST EXILE. They will ask to know which Strozzi, and if I do not say Philippe, nothing will be done.

PIERRE. Imbecile! do as you are told, and only answer for yourself. How do you know beforehand that nothing will be done?

FIRST EXILE. You need not abuse people, my Lord.

PIERRE. Come! mount your horse and go to Sestino.

FIRST EXILE. In fact, my Lord, my horse is tired out. I rode twelve leagues in the night. I have no inclination to saddle him just now.

PIERRE. You are nothing but an idiot. *(To the other exile.)* You go, then; you will go about it better.

SECOND EXILE. Comrade is right as regards Philippe; it is certain that his name would do much for the cause.

PIERRE. Cowards! faint-hearted clodhoppers! Those who would do most for the cause, they are your wives and children who are dying of hunger, do you hear? The name of Philippe may fill their mouths, but it will not fill their bellies. What pigs you are!

SECOND EXILE. It is impossible to come to any understanding with a man as coarse as that. Come on, comrade!

PIERRE. Go to the devil, scoundrels! and tell your confederates, if they have no use for me, that the King of France has; and they had better take care lest I be given authority over all of you!

SECOND EXILE. Come, comrade, let us go to supper; I am tired out, like you.

(Exeunt.)

SCENE IX

(A public square; it is night. Enter Lorenzo.)

LORENZO. I will tell him that it is because of modesty, and I will take away the light. That happens every day; a bride, for example, exacts that of her husband before entering the nuptial chamber, and Catherine poses as very virtuous. Poor girl! who under the sun is, if she is not? If my mother should die of all this: that is what might happen. And so, that is so much done. Patience! One hour is as good as another; the clock has just struck. If you care for it, however? But no, why should you? Shall I take it away? A candle, if you wish; the first time that a woman yields, that is very simple. Come in, warm yourself a little. Oh, my God! yes, merely the caprice of a young girl. And what reason for thinking of this murder? It will astonish everybody, even Philippe. There you are, with livid face!

(The moon arises.)

LORENZO. If the republicans were men, what a revolution in the city to-morrow! But Pierre is an ambitious man; the Ruccellai only are good for anything. Ah, words, words, everlasting words! If there is a God in heaven, he might well laugh at all of us; in truth it is very funny. O, human prattle! O, great mutilator of corpses! great staver-in of open doors! O, armless man! No, no! I shall not take away the

light. I will go straight to the heart; he shall see himself slain....
Blood of Christ! people will gaze out of their windows to-morrow.
Provided he has not contrived some new breastplate, some coat of
mail. Cursed invention! It is easy to wrestle with God and the devil;
but to wrestle with scraps of old iron lapped one over the other by
the dirty hand of an armorer! I will enter after him; he will lay his
sword there—or there, yes, upon the sofa. As for the affair of
winding the cross-belt around the guard, that is an easy matter. If he
should take a notion to go to bed, that would be the best opportunity.
In bed, sitting down, or standing? Preferably sitting down. I will
begin by leaving. Scoronconcolo is shut up in the study. Then we
come in. I should not like to have him turn his back, however. I will
go straight to him. Well, peace! peace! the hour has arrived. I must
go to some wine shop; I had not noticed that I am taking cold. I will
drink a bottle of wine. No, I won't drink. Where the devil shall I go,
anyway? The wine shops are closed. Is she a good girl? Yes, verily.
In her chemise? Oh, no! I do not think so. Poor Catherine! If my
mother should die because of this, how sad it would be! What if I
had told her my plan, what good would it have done? Instead of
consoling her, it would have made her cry, "Crime, crime!" to her
very last breath. I do not know why I am walking. I am ready to
drop from fatigue. *(He sits down.)* Poor Philippe! a daughter as
beautiful as the day! Once upon a time I sat near her under the
chestnut-tree; her little white hands, how she was working! How
many days I have spent, sitting under the trees! All, what peace!
What a horizon at Cafaggiuolo! How pretty Jeannette, the young
daughter of the concierge was, as she was drying her clothes! How
she chased the goats that came walking over her linen stretched
upon the grass! The white goat with the long slender feet would
always come back.

(A clock strikes.)

LORENZO. Ah! ah! I must go down yonder. Good evening,
favorite! eh, drink with Giomo. Good wine! It would be ludicrous if
he were to take a notion to say to me, "Is your chamber secluded?
Can the people in the vicinity hear anything?" That would be
ludicrous. Ah, that is provided for. Yes, it would be droll if that idea
were to enter his head... I am mistaken in the hour; it is only half
past. What is that light under the church porch? Some one is hewing,
some one is moving stones. It would seem as if those men were
courageous with stone. How they cut, how they hew! They are

making a crucifix. With what ardor they apply themselves to the task! I should like to see their marble cadaver seize them suddenly by the throat. Well, well, what now? I have a most incredible desire to dance. I believe if I were to let myself go, I should hop like a sparrow over all these old plasters and beams. Ah, my favorite! put on your new gloves and a finer costume than that; tra-la-la! make yourself handsome, the bride is beautiful. But, I tell you this in a whisper, look out for her little knife. *(Exit, running.)*

SCENE X

(At the Duke's Palace. The Duke, at supper; Giomo. Enter Cardinal Cibo.)

THE CARDINAL. Beware of Lorenzo, my Lord.

THE DUKE. Ah, it's you, Cardinal! Sit down, and take a glass of wine.

THE CARDINAL. Beware of Lorenzo, Duke. He has been to the Bishop of Marzi this evening, to ask permission to have post-horses for tonight.

THE DUKE. That can not be possible.

THE CARDINAL. I have it from the bishop himself.

THE DUKE. Nonsense! I tell you that I have good reasons for knowing that it can not be so.

THE CARDINAL. It is perhaps impossible to make you believe me; I am fulfilling my duty in warning you.

THE DUKE. If it should be true, what is there appalling in it? Perhaps he is going to Cafaggiuolo.

THE CARDINAL. It is this that is appalling, my Lord; in crossing the square, as I was on my way here, I saw him with my two eyes jumping over plaster and stones like a madman. I called to him, and I am forced to own that his look frightened me. You may be sure that he is maturing some scheme in his head for to-night.

THE DUKE. And why should his schemes be dangerous to me?

THE CARDINAL. Must everything be told, even when one is speaking of a favorite? Learn, then, that he told two people of my acquaintance, openly, upon their terrace, that he would kill you to-night.

THE DUKE. Drink a glass of wine, Cardinal. Do you not know that Renzo is usually drunk by sundown?

(Enter Sir Maurice.)

87

SIR MAURICE. Your Highness, look out for Lorenzo. He told three of my friends this evening that he wanted to kill you to-night.

THE DUKE. You too, brave Maurice, you believe in fairy tales? I thought you more of a man than that.

SIR MAURICE. Your Highness knows whether I am frightened without a cause or not. What I say to you, I can prove.

THE DUKE. Sit down, and take a drink with the Cardinal. You will not take it amiss if I go about my affairs. Well, favorite, it is time already?

(Enter Lorenzo.)

LORENZO. It is just twelve o'clock.

THE DUKE. Give me my sable doublet.

LORENZO. Let us hurry; your beauty is perhaps already at the rendezvous.

THE DUKE. What gloves ought I to take, those of a warrior, or those of a lover?

LORENZO. Those of a lover, your Highness.

THE DUKE. All right; I wish to be a devoted admirer of the sex.

(Exeunt.)

SIR MAURICE. What do you say to that, Cardinal?

THE CARDINAL. That the will of God is done in spite of men.

(Exeunt.)

SCENE XI

(Lorenzo's Chamber. Enter the Duke and Lorenzo.)

THE DUKE. I am frozen; it is indeed cold. *(He takes off his sword.)* Well, favorite, what-are you doing now?

LORENZO. I am winding your cross-belt around your sword, and I will put it under your pillow. It is always well to have a weapon at hand.

(He winds the cross-belt in a manner to prevent the sword from coming out of the scabbard.)

THE DUKE. You know that I hate prattling, and I recall that Catherine used to be a good talker. To avoid conversation, I am going to bed. By the by, why did you order post-horses of the Bishop of Marzi.

LORENZO. To go and see my brother who is very ill, as he wrote me.

THE DUKE. Go now to seek your aunt.

LORENZO. In a moment. *(Exit.)*

THE DUKE *(alone)*. To pay court to a woman who answers yes to you, when she is asked yes or no, has always appeared to me very foolish, and altogether worthy of a Frenchman. To-day, especially, when I have eaten supper enough for three monks, I would be incapable of even saying, "My heart!" or "My sweet love!" to the Spanish infanta herself. I will pretend to be asleep: it will not be very gallant, perhaps, but it will be agreeable. *(He goes to bed.)*

(Lorenzo returns, sword in hand.)

LORENZO. Are you asleep, my Lord?

(He stabs him.)

THE DUKE. Is that you, Renzo?

LORENZO. My Lord, have no doubt of it. *(He stabs him again.)*

(Enter Scoronconcolo.)

SCORONCONCOLO. Is it done?

LORENZO. Look, he has bitten my finger. I will preserve this bloody ring as a priceless gem to my dying day.

SCORONCONCOLO. Ah, my God! it is the Duke of Florence.

LORENZO *(seating himself at the window)*. What a beautiful night! How pure the air of heaven is! Breathe, breathe, heart broken with joy!

SCORONCONCOLO. Come, master, we have done too much; let us fly.

LORENZO. How soft and balmy the evening air is! How the flowers of the fields are bursting their buds! O, magnificent nature! O, eternal repose!

SCORONCONCOLO. The wind will freeze the sweat which is trickling down your face. Come, my Lord.

LORENZO. Ah, God of love! what a moment!

SCORONCONCOLO *(aside)*. His mind expands strangely. As for me, I shall take time by the forelock. *(He starts to leave.)*

LORENZO. Wait; draw those curtains. Now give me the key to this chamber.

SCORONCONCOLO. Provided the neighbors have heard nothing!

LORENZO. Do not you remember that they are accustomed to our racket? Come, let us go.

(Exeunt.)

ACT THE FIFTH

SCENE I

(At the Duke's Palace. Enter Valori, Sir Maurice and Guicciardini. A crowd of courtiers circulate about the salon and grounds of the Palace.)

SIR MAURICE. Giomo has not yet returned from his errand; this is becoming more and more disquieting.

GUICCIARDINI. There he is, coming into the salon.

(Enter Giomo.)

SIR MAURICE. Well, what did you find out?

GIOMO. Nothing at all. *(Exit.)*

GUICCIARDINI. He doesn't wish to reply; Cardinal Cibo is secluded in the Duke's study; the news only comes to him.

(Enter another messenger).

GUICCIARDINI. Well, has the Duke been found? Does any one know what has become of him?

THE MESSENGER. I do not know. *(He goes into the study.)*

VALORI. What a dreadful thing, gentlemen, this disappearance! No news of the Duke yet! Didn't you say, Sir Maurice, that you saw him last evening? Did he appear to be ill?

(Reenter Giomo.)

GIOMO *(to Sir Maurice)*. I must whisper it to you: the Duke is assassinated.

SIR MAURICE. Assassinated! By whom? Where did you find him?

GIOMO. Where you told us: in Lorenzo's chamber.

SIR MAURICE. Ah, devil's blood! Does the Cardinal know it?

GIOMO. Yes, my Lord.

SIR MAURICE. What has he decided? What is to be done about it? The people are crowding before the palace already; all this hideous affair has come to pass. We are dead men if it is confirmed; they will massacre us!

(Valets carrying casks of wine and baskets of food, pass in the background.)

GUICCIARDINI. What does that mean? Are they going to make distributions to the people?

(Enter a courtier.)

THE COURTIER. Is the Duke at leisure, gentlemen? This is my cousin, just arrived from Germany, whom I desire to present to his Lordship; be kind enough to look upon him with favor.

GUICCIARDINI. Answer him, Sir Valori; I don't know what to say to him.

VALORI. The salon is filling up every moment with these morning flatterers. They are waiting patiently to be admitted.

SIR MAURICE *(to Giomo)*. Has he been concealed?

GIOMO. Yes, indeed, in the sacristy. It can't be helped! If the people were to learn of this death it would be the cause of many more. In due time he will be given a public funeral. Meanwhile we brought him away in a rug.

VALORI. What will become of us?

SEVERAL COURTIERS *(drawing near)*. Will we soon be permitted to pay our respects to his Highness? What do you think about it, gentlemen?

CARDINAL CIBO *(entering)*. Yes, gentlemen, you may go in in an hour or two; the Duke passed the night at a masquerade, and he is resting just now.

(The valets hang dominos at the casements.)

THE COURTIERS. Let us withdraw; the Duke is still in bed. He passed the night at a ball.

(Exeunt Courtiers. Enter the Eight.)

NICCOLINI. Well, Cardinal, what has been decided?

THE CARDINAL. Primo avulso non deficit alter—Aurens, et simili frondescit virga metallo. *(Exit.)*

NICCOLINI. That's all very fine! but what has that to do with it? The Duke is dead; another must be chosen, and that as soon as possible. If we have not a duke by this evening, or to-morrow, it is all up with us. The people are in a ferment just now.

VETTORI. I propose Octavien de Medicis.

CAPPONI. Why? He is not the first choice by right of birth.

ACCIAIUIOLI. We might take the Cardinal.

SIR MAURICE. Are you joking?

RUCCELLAI. Why, in fact, should you not take the Cardinal, since you have allowed him, contrary to all law, to declare himself sole judge in this affair?

VETTORI. He is a man capable of directing it well.

RUCCELLAI. Let him get an order from the Pope.

VETTORI. He has done that; the Pope sent the authority by a messenger whom the Cardinal despatched in the night.

RUCCELLAI. You mean by a bird, doubtless; for a messenger must take time to go, before taking it to return. Do they take us for children?

CANIGIANI *(approaching).* Gentlemen, if you will take my advice, this is what we will do: we will elect his natural son, Julian, Duke of Florence.

RUCCELLAI. Bravo! a child five years old! Isn't he five years old, Canigiani?

GUICCIARDINI *(low).* Don't you see the point? It was the Cardinal who put that foolish notion into his head: Cibo would be regent, and the child would eat sweetmeats.

RUCCELLAI. This is shameful! I shall leave the room, if you keep on talking like this.

CORSI *(entering).* Gentlemen, the Cardinal has just written to Cosmo de Medicis.

THE EIGHT. Without consulting us?

CORSI. The Cardinal has likewise written to Pisa, to Arezzo, and to Pistoja, to the military commanders. Jacques de Medicis will be here to-morrow, with as large a force as possible. Alexander Vitelli is already in the fortress with the entire garrison. As for Lorenzo, he has despatched three messengers to overtake him.

RUCCELLAI. Your Cardinal had better proclaim himself duke at once, and have done with it.

CORSI. He ordered me to beg of you to put the election of Cosmo de Medicis to vote, under the provisional title of Governor of the Florentine Republic.

GIOMO *(to the valets who cross the salon).* Distribute drinks at the door, and don't spare the wine more than the rest.

RUCCELLAI. Poor people... what idlers they are making of you!

SIR MAURICE. Come, gentlemen, to vote. Here are your ballots.

FETTORI. Cosmo is indeed the first by right after Alexander; he is his nearest relative.

ACCIAIUOLI. What kind of a man is he? I know him very slightly.

CORSI. He is the best prince in the world.

GUICCIARDINI. Ah, ah, not altogether that. If you were to say, the most expansive and polite of princes, it would be nearer the truth.

SIR MAURICE. Your votes, gentlemen!

RUCCELLAI. I formally object to this vote, for myself, and in the name of all the citizens.

FETTORI. Why?

RUCCELLAI. The Republic no longer needs either princes, or dukes, or lords. Here is my vote!

(He shows a blank ballot.)

VETTORI. Your vote is only one vote. We can do without you.

RUCCELLAI. Farewell then; I wash my hands of it.

GUICCIARDINI *(running after him)*. Ah, my God! Palla, you are too hasty.

RUCCELLAI. Leave me alone; I am more than sixty-two years old, therefore you can do me no great harm in future. *(Exit.)*

NICCOLINI. Your votes, gentlemen! *(He unfolds the ballots thrown into a hat.)* It is unanimous. Has the messenger left for Trebbio?

CORSI. Yes, my lord. Cosmo will be here tomorrow afternoon; at least, if he doesn't decline.

VETTORI. Why should he decline?

NICCOLINI. Ah, my God! if he should decline, what would become of us? Fifteen leagues from here to Trebbio to find Cosmo, and as many to return, would be a day lost. We ought to have chosen some one who was nearer.

VETTORI. It can't be helped! Our vote is cast, and it is probable that he will accept. This is all very amazing.

(Exeunt.)

SCENE II

(At Venice. Philippe Strozzi in his study.)

PHILIPPE. I am told that Pierre is in correspondence with the King of France; that he is at the head of an army, and ready to put the city to fire and sword. This, then, is what will be done with this poor name of Strozzi, which has been so long respected! It will have produced a rebel and two or three massacres. O, my Louise! you are sleeping peacefully beneath the sod; the oblivion of the whole world is around about you, as within you, in the depths of the somber valley where I left you. *(Some one knocks at the door.)* Come in!

(Enter Lorenzo.)

LORENZO. Philippe! I bring you the most beautiful jewel of your crown.

PHILIPPE. What is that you threw there—a key?

LORENZO. That key opens the door of my chamber, and in my chamber is Alexander de Medicis, dead by this hand which I show you.

PHILIPPE. Truly! truly! This is incredible.

LORENZO. Believe it, if you wish. You will know it from others besides me.

PHILIPPE *(taking the key)*. Alexander is dead! Is it possible?

LORENZO. What would you say if the republicans should offer you the title of Duke in his place?

PHILIPPE. I should refuse it, my friend.

LORENZO. Truly! truly! That is incredible.

PHILIPPE. Why? It is very simple to me.

LORENZO. As for me to kill Alexander. Why don't you believe me?

PHILIPPE. Oh, our new Brutus! I believe you, and I embrace you. Liberty is saved! Yes, I believe you; you are like what you told me you were. Give me your hand. The Duke is dead! Ah, there is no hatred in my joy; there is only love, the purest, the most holy, for my country. I call upon God as my witness!

LORENZO. Come, calm yourself; there is nothing saved but me, and I have my back broken by the Bishop of Marzi's horses.

PHILIPPE. Didn't you notify our friends? Are they not armed by this time?

LORENZO. I did notify them; I knocked at all republican doors with the diligence of a brother-seeker; I told them to polish their swords, for Alexander would be dead when they awakened. I think by this time that they have awakened more than once, and slept again at pleasure. But, indeed, I don't suppose they would do anything else.

PHILIPPE. Did you notify the Pazzis? Did you tell it to Corsini?

LORENZO. To everybody. I might as well have said it to the moon, so sure was I that they paid no attention to what I said.

PHILIPPE. What do you mean by that?

LORENZO. I mean that they shrugged their shoulders and returned to their dinners, their dice-boxes, and their women.

PHILIPPE. Didn't you explain the affair to them?

LORENZO. What the devil would you have me explain? Do you think that I had an hour to lose with each one of them? I said to them, "Prepare yourselves," and I did my deed.

PHILIPPE. And you believe that the Pazzis are doing nothing? What do you know about it? You have had no news since you left, and you were several days coming here.

LORENZO. I believe that the Pazzis are doing something; I believe that they are fencing in their ante-chamber, and drinking wine from time to time, whenever their throats are dry.

PHILIPPE. You are not sustaining your wager; didn't you want to bet me that what you are saying would be the case? Don't be mean! I am more hopeful than you.

LORENZO. I am more easy than I can tell.

PHILIPPE. Why didn't you carry the Duke's head through the streets? The people would have followed you as their savior and their chief.

LORENZO. I left the stag to the hounds; let them eat up the quarry.

PHILIPPE. You would have deified men, if you did not despise them.

LORENZO. I don't despise them; I know them; I am fully persuaded that there are very few who are very bad, many cowards, and a great many indifferent ones among them. There are also ferocious ones, like the inhabitants of Pistoja, who have found in this affair an occasion for cutting the throats of all their chancellors in broad daylight, in the middle of the streets. I learned that not an hour ago.

PHILIPPE. I am filled with joy and hope; my heart beats high in spite of me.

LORENZO. So much the better for you.

PHILIPPE. Since you know nothing about it, why do you speak about it as you do? To be sure, all men are not capable of great things, but all are sensible of great things: do you deny the history of the whole world? Doubtless a spark is needed to fire a forest; but the spark may be struck by a stone, and the forest take fire. It is thus that the flash of a single saber may illuminate an entire century.

LORENZO. I don't deny history, but I wasn't there.

PHILIPPE. Let me call you Brutus; if I am a dreamer, leave me that dream. Oil, my friends, my compatriots! you can make a fine death-bed for the old Strozzis if you choose.

LORENZO. Why do you open the window?

PHILIPPE. Don't you see a messenger coming? My Brutus! my grand Lorenzo! liberty is in the air; I feel it, I breathe it.

LORENZO. Philippe! Philippe! none of that; close your window; all these words make me sick.

PHILIPPE. It seems to me that there is a mob in the street; a town-crier is reading a proclamation. Hallo, Jean! go and buy the paper of that crier.

LORENZO. O, God! O, God!

PHILIPPE. You're as pale as death! What is the matter with you?

LORENZO. Didn't you hear anything?

(Enter a servant bringing the proclamation.)

PHILIPPE. No; read this paper that they were hawking in the street.

LORENZO *(reading).* "To any man, noble or plebeian, who will kill Lorenzo de Medicis, a traitor to his country and the assassin of his master, in whatever place and by whatever means it may be, throughout all Italy, the Council of the Eight at Florence promise the following reward: 1. Four thousand gold florins net; 2. An annuity of one hundred gold florins, to be given to him during his life, and to his direct descendants after his death. 3. Permission to exercise all the offices of a magistrate, to possess all benefits and privileges of the state, in spite of his birth if he is a plebeian. 4. A perpetual pardon for all his errors, past and future, ordinary or extraordinary. Signed by the Hand of the Eight."... Well, Philippe! you wouldn't believe just now that I had killed Alexander. You see now that I did kill him.

PHILIPPE. Hush! somebody is coming up the stairs. Hide yourself in that chamber.

(Exeunt.)

SCENE III

(Florence, A street. Enter two noblemen.)

FIRST NOBLEMAN. Isn't that the Marquis of Cibo who is coming? It appears that he is walking arm-in-arm with his wife.

(The Marquis and Marquise pass.)

SECOND NOBLEMAN. It seems that this good Marquis is not of a vindictive nature. Who is there in Florence that doesn't know that his wife was the mistress of the late Duke?

FIRST NOBLEMAN. They appear to be very well reconciled. I thought I saw them squeezing hands.

SECOND NOBLEMAN. The pearl of husbands, indeed! He must have a very strong stomach to be able to swallow that.

FIRST NOBLEMAN. I know that it makes talk; however, I should advise you not to go to him and talk about it to his face. He is a good match for any one with all kinds of weapons, and scandal-mongers fear the vials of his wrath.

SECOND NOBLEMAN. He is a queer fellow, there is no use talking.

(Exeunt.)

SCENE IV

(A tavern. Enter Pierre Strozzi and a Messenger.)

PIERRE. These are his own words?
THE MESSENGER. Yes, my Lord; the King's own words.
PIERRE. Very well.

(Exit Messenger.)

PIERRE. The King of France protecting the liberty of Italy is, in fact, like a thief protecting a pretty woman against another thief. He protects her until he has violated her. However that may be, a path is opening before me, upon which there is more wheat than chaff. A curse upon that Lorenzaccio, who thinks he's somebody! My revenge slipped through my fingers like a frightened bird. I can imagine nothing here that is worthy of me. Let us make a vigorous attack upon the town, and then have done with these old women who think of nothing but the name of my father, and who eye me the livelong day from head to foot, to discover wherein I resemble him. I was born for something besides a leader of bandits. *(Exit.)*

SCENE V

(A square. Florence. The Goldsmith and the Mercer.)

THE MERCER. Mark what I tell you; pay attention to my words. The late Duke Alexander was killed in the year 1536, this present year. Follow me carefully. He was killed, then, in 1536; so much for that. He was twenty-six years old; do you grasp that? But that is not all. He was twenty-six years old, then; right! He died the sixth of the month; ah, ah! did you know that? Was it not just the sixth of the month that he died? Listen now. He died at six o'clock in the evening. What do you think of that, Father Mondella? If that isn't extraordinary, I don't know what is. He died, then, at six o'clock in the evening. Keep still! don't say anything yet. He had six wounds. Very well! have you made a note of that? He had six wounds; at six o'clock in the evening, the sixth of the month, at twenty-six years of age, in the year 1536. Now, one word more: he had reigned six years.

THE GOLDSMITH. What nonsense are you giving me, neighbor?

THE MERCER. What! what! are you absolutely incapable of calculating? You don't see what has been the result of these supernatural combinations which I have the honor of explaining to you.

THE GOLDSMITH. No, indeed, I don't see the result of it.

THE MERCER. You don't see it? Is it possible, neighbor, that you don't see it?

THE GOLDSMITH. I don't see that the least thing results from it. What use could it be to us?

THE MERCER. The result is that six sixes have contributed to the death of Alexander. Hush! don't repeat this as coming from me. You know that I am regarded as a wise and circumspect man; don't do me any harm, in the name of all the saints! It is a more serious matter than you think; I till it to you in confidence.

THE GOLDSMITH. Go about your business; I am an old man, but not an old granny yet. Cosmo arrives to-day, which is the most apparent result of our affair; there has sprung for us a fine splitter of words in your night of six sixes. Ah, death in life! isn't it a shame! My workmen, neighbor, to the last man, rapped upon their blocks with their tools, upon seeing the Eight pass, and shouted to them: "If you don't know enough, and can't take action, call upon us, who will act."

THE MERCER. Your workmen were not the only ones that shouted; there is a hubbub in the city such as was never before heard of.

THE GOLDSMITH. The people are clamoring for a vote; some are running after the soldiers, others after the wine that is being dispensed; they fill their mouths and brains with it, so that they lose what little common sense and decent speech that might remain to them.

THE MERCER. There are some who would like to reestablish the Council, and boldly elect a gonfalonière, as in days of old.

THE GOLDSMITH. There are some who would like to, as you say, but there are none who have taken any steps to bring it about. As old as I am, I went to the market-place, and received the thrust of a halberd in my leg, because I demanded a vote. Not a soul came to my rescue. Nobody but The Students showed themselves.

THE MERCER. I can readily believe that. Do you know what they say, neighbor? They say that the purveyor, Roberto Corsini, went last evening to the republican meeting, at the Salviati palace.

THE GOLDSMITH. Nothing is truer than that. He offered to deliver the fortress to the friends of liberty, with the supplies, keys, and all the rest.

THE MERCER. Did he do it, neighbor—did he do that? It is a treason against high justice!

THE GOLDSMITH. Yes, indeed! They have brawled, drunk sweet wine, smashed windowpanes; but the proposition of that brave man was not even listened to. Because they didn't dare do what he wished them to, they said they distrusted him, and that they suspected him of treachery in his offers. By all the devils in Hades, how mad it makes me! Look the messengers from Trebbio are coming! Cosmo isn't far away. Good night, neighbor, I can't keep still! I must go to the palace. *(Exit.)*

THE MERCER. Wait for me, neighbor; I will go with you. *(Exit.)*

(Enter a preceptor with the little Salviati boy, and another with the little Strozzi boy.)

FIRST PRECEPTOR. Sapientissime Doctor, how is your Lordship? Is the treasure of your precious health in its usual state, and your equipoise properly maintained in these tempestuous times?

SECOND PRECEPTOR. A weighty matter, my Lord Doctor, is an encounter as learned and as flowery as yours upon this cracked and careworn earth. Permit me to press that gigantic hand, whence have sprung the masterpieces of our language. Confess it, you composed a sonnet recently.

YOUNG SALVIATI. Brat of a Strozzi that you are!

YOUNG STROZZI. Your father got a licking, Salviati.

FIRST PRECEPTOR. Has the poor sport of our muse reached as far as you, who are such a conscientious man of art, so rigid and so austere? Eyes like yours which play upon such serrated and phosphorescent horizons, have they consented to occupy themselves with vapors, perchance fantastical and bold, of an iridescent imagination?

SECOND PRECEPTOR. Oh! if you love art, and if you love us, I pray you, recite to us your sonnet. The city is occupied with nothing but your sonnet.

FIRST PRECEPTOR. You will perhaps be surprised that I, who began by singing the monarchy after a fashion, seem this time to sing the republic.

YOUNG SALVIATI. Stop kicking me, Strozzi!

YOUNG STROZZI. There, dog of a Salviati, there are two more!

FIRST PRECEPTOR. These are the verses:

> Let us sing of liberty, which flourishes
> More ardently…

YOUNG SALVIATI. Make this gamin stop, sir; he's a ruffian! All the Strozzis are ruffians!

SECOND PRECEPTOR. See here, boy, you be quiet!

YOUNG STROZZI. You are always doing things on the sly! There, rascal, take that to your father, and tell him to put it with the gash which he received from Pierre Strozzi, poisoner that you are! You are all poisoners!

FIRST PRECEPTOR. Will you shut up, mischievous child? *(He slaps him.)*

YOUNG STROZZI. Oh! oh! he slapped me!

FIRST PRECEPTOR.

> Let us sing of liberty, which flourishes
> More ardently 'neath riper suns and skies
> More fair...

YOUNG STROZZI. Oh! oh! he has skinned my ear!

SECOND PRECEPTOR. You struck too hard, my friend.

(Young Strozzi pounds young Salviati.)

FIRST PRECEPTOR. Well, what does it all mean?

SECOND PRECEPTOR. Go on, I beg of you.

FIRST PRECEPTOR. I would, with pleasure, but these children won't stop beating each other.

(Exeunt children, quarreling; the preceptors follow them.)

SCENE VI

(Florence. A street. Enter Students and Soldiers.)

A STUDENT. Since the great lords use only their tongues, let us use our arms. Hallo! the votes! the votes! Citizens of Florence, don't let a duke be elected without a vote.

A SOLDIER. You will have no votes. Be off!

THE STUDENT. Citizens, come here. He has menaced your rights, he is insulting the people.

(A great tumult.)

THE SOLDIERS. Out of the way! Be off!

ANOTHER STUDENT. We will die for our rights.

A SOLDIER. Die then! *(He stabs him.)*

THE STUDENT. Avenge me, Roberto, and comfort my mother! *(He dies.)*

(The students attack the soldiers; they retire fighting.)

SCENE VII

(Venice. Strozzi's study. Enter Philippe and Lorenzo, holding a letter.)

LORENZO. Here is a letter which informs me that my mother is dead. Come and take a little walk, Philippe.

PHILIPPE. I beg of you, my friend, not to tempt fate. You go and come continually, as if that proclamation of death did not exist against you.

LORENZO. At the time I was going to kill Clement VII, a price was put upon my head in Rome; it is natural for it to be so throughout Italy, now that I have killed Alexander. If I were to leave Italy, I should presently be trumpeted throughout all Europe, and at my death the good God would not fail to have my eternal damnation placarded at all the cross-roads of space.

PHILIPPE. Your humor is as sad as death. You have not changed, Lorenzo.

LORENZO. No, indeed; I wear the same clothes, I always walk upon my legs, and I yawn with my mouth; there is nothing changed in me but a misery; that is, that I am more hollow and more empty than a tin statue.

PHILIPPE. Let us go away together. Become a man again. You have been guilty of many things, but you are young yet.

LORENZO. I am older than Methuselah. I pray you, come for a walk.

PHILIPPE. Your mind tortures itself in inactivity; that is your misfortune. You have whims, my friend.

LORENZO. I admit that. That the republicans have done nothing at Florence, that is a great whim on my part. That a hundred brave and determined young students have been butchered in vain; that Cosmo, a mere clodhopper, has been unanimously elected—oh! I confess, I confess those are unpardonable whims, which do me the greatest wrong.

PHILIPPE. Let us not argue over an event which has not come to pass. The most important thing is to get out of Italy. You have not yet finished your earthly career.

LORENZO. I was a machine of murder, but of only one murder.

PHILIPPE. Have you not been happy aside from this murder? Even though you should only live as an honest man, as an artist, henceforth, why should you want to die?

LORENZO. I can only repeat my own words to you: I used to be virtuous. Perhaps I might become so again, were it not for the ennui which seizes me. I still love women and wine; that is enough, it is true, to make a rake of me, but not enough to make me want to be one. Let us go out, I beg of you!

PHILIPPE. You will get yourself killed in some of these walks.

LORENZO. It amuses me to be stalked. The reward is so great that it almost makes people courageous. Yesterday, a tall fellow with bare legs followed me along the edge of the water for a quarter of an hour, without being able to resolve upon killing me. The poor man carried some kind of a knife as long as a boar's tusk; he looked at it with such a sheepish air that I pitied him; perhaps he was the father of a family which was dying of hunger.

PHILIPPE. O, Lorenzo, Lorenzo! you are very sick at heart. He was doubtless an honest man; why attribute to people's cowardice their respect for the unfortunate?

LORENZO. Attribute it to whatever you please. I am going to take a turn on the Rialto. *(Exit.)*

PHILIPPE. I must have some one of my people follow him. Hallo, Jean! Pippo! hallo!

(Enter a servant.)

PHILIPPE. Take a sword, you and one of your comrades, and follow Signor Lorenzo at a suitable distance, so as to be able to go to his assistance if anybody attacks him.

JEAN. Yes, my Lord.

(Enter Pippo.)

PIPPO. My Lord, Lorenzo is dead! A man was hidden behind the door, who stabbed him from behind as he was going out.

PHILIPPE. Let us hurry; perhaps he is only wounded.

PIPPO. Don't you see all that mob? The people have thrown themselves upon him. Merciful God! they are throwing the body into the lagoon!

PHILIPPE. How horrible! how horrible! What, not even a tomb! *(Exit.)*

SCENE VIII

(Florence. The great square. The public galleries are filled with people.)

THE CROWD. *(running from all sides.)* The votes! the votes! He is the Duke! He is the Duke! The votes! He is the Duke of Florence!

THE SOLDIERS. Be off with you, rascals!

CARDINAL CIBO *(upon a stage, to Cosmo de Medicis).* My Lord, you are Duke of Florence. Before receiving from my hands the crown which the Pope and the Emperor have charged me to confer upon you, I am commanded to have you take four oaths.

COSMO. What are they, Cardinal?

THE CARDINAL. To administer justice without reservation; never to attempt anything against the authority of Charles V; to avenge the death of Alexander; and to be kind to Signor Jules and Signorina Julia, his natural children.

COSMO. How must I take this oath?

THE CARDINAL. Upon the Bible. *(He presents him the Bible.)* I swear before God, and you, Cardinal. Now give me your hand.

(They advance toward the people. Cosmo is heard speaking in the background.)

COSMO. "Most Noble and Most Puissant Lords, the return which I would make to your most illustrious and most gracious Lordships, for the great benefits which I owe to you, is none other than the pledge which is most agreeable to me, that young as I am, to have always before my eyes, along with the fear of God, honesty and justice, and the intention to injure no man, either in his estates or in his honor; and as to the government of affairs, never to deviate from the counsel and judgment of their most prudent and judicious Lordships, to whom I present myself entirely, and commend myself most devoutly."

(End of Lorenzaccio.)

CPSIA information can be obtained at www.ICGtesting.com
Printed in the USA
LVOW07s1529080116

469780LV00015B/159/P